I0642216

Franz Xavier Weniger

The Perfect Religious According to the Rule of St. Augustine

Insructions

Franz Xavier Weniger

The Perfect Religious According to the Rule of St. Augustine
Insructions

ISBN/EAN: 9783744659345

Printed in Europe, USA, Canada, Australia, Japan

Cover: Foto ©Lupo / pixelio.de

More available books at **www.hansebooks.com**

THE PERFECT RELIGIOUS.

THE PERFECT RELIGIOUS

ACCORDING TO THE

Rule of St. Augustine:

OR

INSTRUCTIONS FOR ALL RELIGIOUS,

REFERRING PRINCIPALLY TO THE CONSTITUTIONS OF RELIGIOUS URSULINES.

BY

FATHER FRANCIS- XAVIER WENIGER,

PRIEST OF THE SOCIETY OF JESUS.

TRANSLATED FROM THE GERMAN

A MEMBER OF THE URSULINE COMMUNITY.
ST. MARY'S, WATERFORD,

"Fulfil all the words that are written in this law ; for they are not commanded you in vain."—DEUT. xxxii. 46, 47.

DUBLIN:

M. H. GILL AND SON,

O'CONNELL STREET

1888

Nihil Obstat :

P. J. TYNAN, S.T.D.,

Censor Theol. Deput.

Imprimatur :

✠ GULIELMUS J. WALSH,

Archiepiscopus Dublinensis
Hiberniæ Primas.

THE AUTHOR'S PREFACE.

Of the many Monastic Rules which have been approved by the Church of God, the Rule of St. Augustine is specially distinguished by remarkable proofs of the virtue it possesses for leading souls to the highest perfection, according to the letter and the spirit of the Gospel.

Numerous communities, belonging to different orders, have chosen it in preference to others, because it so admirably combines evangelic austerity with the sweet spirit of our Saviour Jesus Christ.

It seems particularly suited to those Orders of Religious Women, who, while labouring for their own sanctification, devote themselves to the instruction of youth. Among these it has been adopted by the Ursulines, and the Daugh-

ters of St. Francis de Sales, institutes that are
conspicuous in the Church for the zeal with
which they endeavour to promote the glory of
God.

But as in its quality of a Rule, it is necessarily brief, the need of some explanation
having regard to existing times and circumstances has long been felt. This want I hope
to meet by the present little work. As the
most urgent entreaties to undertake it have
come to me from Ursuline Communities, I
naturally take their Holy Constitutions as the
ground-work of the Commentary, which, however, I have composed in such a manner as that
it may also suit Religious of kindred Orders.

May the Almighty bestow His richest blessings on this seed of His Word, which is
destined to germinate and flourish in so
privileged a soil.

F. X. WENIGER, S.J.

CONTENTS.

———◆———

THE
PERFECT RELIGIOUS,

ACCORDING TO THE RULE OF OUR HOLY FATHER,

ST. AUGUSTINE.

---◆---

CHAPTER I.

OF THE END AND SPIRIT OF THE INSTITUTE.

"Before all things, my dear Sisters, love God and then your neighbour ; for these two commandments have been principally given unto us."

LOVE GOD.

According to the unanimous doctrine of the holy Fathers, and of theologians, the virtues are divided into theological and moral. The former are so named, because God is their immediate object; they are Faith, Hope, and Charity. All the others, having as immediate object the regulation and sanctification of our conduct in our social relations, are, for this reason, called moral virtues. The queen of

2

these virtues is charity, without this all the rest are as if they were not, losing their value and supernatural merit before God. Therefore, the great apostle says: *If I speak with the tongues of angels, . . . and if I should have all faith, so that I could remove mountains, and have not charity, I am nothing.*[1] And elsewhere, supporting the testimony of the Apostle of Charity, the beloved St. John, he tells us that *Love is the fulfilment of the law.*[2] And Jesus Christ Himself teaches us that love is the abridgment and the accomplishment of the law. *On these two commandments dependeth the whole law and the prophets.*[3]

Justly, then, do the constitutions of the Rule of our Holy Father begin with this sublime and praiseworthy virtue. Let us briefly consider its essence and exercise in relation to the religious state, and particularly as regards the daughters of St. Angela.

To state its essence and to define it, we say that it is a virtue infused by God, and by which we love God above all things for Himself, and our neighbour as ourselves, for the love of God.

---

[1] 1 Cor. xiii. 1, 2.   [2] Rom. xiii. 10.   [3] St. Matt. xxii. 40.

Hence are derived consequences of the highest importance for the end at which we aim.

In the first place, charity is a virtue inspired by God. Let us, then, often ardently and perseveringly pray Him to pour it more and more abundantly into our hearts. Let us beg for it in that perfect degree that will make us love God above all, not so much because we are indebted to Him, the liberal dispenser of every best gift, for all that we are, and all that we have; as, because He, being the supreme and sovereign good, merits to be loved for His own sake, and to be loved before all, with our whole heart, with our whole soul, with all our mind, and with all our strength; and that, at all times and everywhere, He merits our most devoted and loving service.

Those from whom God chiefly desires this worship of love are the souls consecrated to Him by the blessed vows of religion; and belonging to Him so specially as they do, who are more bound than they to fulfil this duty perfectly? The mind of the Spouse of Christ is dedicated to the love of God by the frequent and fervent meditations she makes on His sovereign perfections, learning thus to esteem Him infinitely more than all created things, and, consequently, more than all she has quitted for His love—father, mother, brothers, sisters, friends, and fortune.

What, then, would be the crime and folly of a religious, who, after renouncing secular life, should return to it in spirit, considering it with the eyes of her mind, and permitting herself to be anxious and troubled about secular affairs; or, of another, who, responding to the call of her Lord, had contemned whatever the world could give or offer, and who, nevertheless, after all these sacrifices, would attach herself in the convent to a book, a picture, a cell, a beads, a habit, or the like, and cling to these insignificant objects more tenaciously than she would in the world to possessions of some importance? Never will such religious attain to perfect charity.

The memory of a Spouse of Christ is consecrated to the love of God by her habitual thought of Him and by walking constantly in His presence. She should strive for the spirit of recollection; for, without it, devotion infallibly grows cold. Nor should she fail to exercise memory in the love of her adorable

Master by a grateful recollection of His immense and innumerable benefits, and especially for the gift of the true faith and the grace of her sublime vocation.

There can be no doubt that often-repeated thanks for the happiness of the religious vocation, is a powerful stimulus to the love of God. We know that the Fathers of the monastic life were accustomed to solemnize the anniversaries of their profession.

Guided by the same spirit, the daughters of St. Angela have retreats prescribed to them by their Constitutions, as times destined for particular recollection and renovation ; and, by bringing to those days of grace hearts all-thankful for their holy vocation, they are certain to make extraordinary progress in divine love.

The Spouse of Christ should love God with all the strength of her will ; and by means of this power of the soul she ought generously and faithfully:

1. To perform all her actions for the pure love of God.
2. Through the same motive to perform them as perfectly as possible.

3. To keep the ear of her heart ever attentive to the Divine inspirations, in order
to profit by every opportunity of serving God and leading others to serve
Him. For this end she can offer her
prayers and penances, and thus draw
down abundant graces upon preachers,
confessors, and, in a word, upon all who
labour in the vineyard of the Lord, to
guide, extend, and protect His Church.

This pure intention, often renewed, this offer-
ing of every act, and even of every step, made
repeatedly during the day, will add new flames
to the sacred fire. Our very bodies will be immolated to this holy love by the sacrifice of obedience; for, since all that we do is done solely
through charity and obedience, it follows that
we neither see, nor hear, sleep, eat, labour, or
make use of any sense or faculty, but in the
service of God, and as victims of His love.

With all her heart, then, let the Spouse of
Christ exercise herself in producing holy and
fervent affections, loving God supremely, and
loving herself and all else only in God, and for
God, so that she may be able to repeat with
truth from her inmost soul the words of the

Spouse in the Canticles: *My Beloved is all mine, and I am all His.*[1] Then will she rejoice in God and in His infinite perfections more than in her own existence, and exult with joy as she joins the Holy Church in chanting at the *Gloria* of the Mass these wondrous words: *We give Thee thanks, O God, for Thy great glory.* Moreover, she will be ready to testify her love, not only by voluntary deeds, but likewise by her endurance of all the temptations, tribulations, and sufferings whereby God is pleased to try devout souls, and particularly His chosen Spouses.

Far from being weakened by this trial, true charity is nourished as fire is by oil. *Its light is a flame of fire. Many waters cannot quench charity, ... and if a man should give all the substance of his house for love, he shall despise it as nothing.*[2]

This exhortation to love is of the more importance to the religious, as she should be intimately persuaded that if the way of the cross is for all the royal road of salvation, it is so in a most peculiar manner for those who are specially consecrated to the imitation of Jesus, and the service of God. Let them, therefore, be prepared for temptations and crosses of many

[1] Cant. ii. 16.   [2] Cant. viii. 6, 7.

kinds, for such infallibly await them. But none should be discouraged. Souls that truly love never feel dismayed; they sustain no injury, whatever may be the weight or number of their trials. Like St. Paul, they glory in the Cross of their Beloved, and superabounding with consolations, they exclaim in the midst of their sufferings : *Who then shall separate us from the love of Christ? Shall tribulation, or distress, or famine, or nakedness, or danger, or persecution? No—for I am sure that neither death nor life, nor angels, nor things present, nor things to come, nor height, nor depth, nor any other creature shall be able to separate us from the love of God, which is in Christ Jesus, our Lord,* unto whom I am consecrated for time and eternity, as a victim of the most generous, tender, and faithful love.[1]

It was thus that St. Angela loved God with her understanding, memory, and will; with her whole heart and soul, and with all her strength, as a true daughter of St. Augustine, styled " the Seraphical Father." And justly is so sublime a title bestowed on this holy doctor,

[1] Rom. viii. 38, 39.

who in one of his transports of love exclaimed :
" Were I God, and God, Augustine, I would be
Augustine that God might be God ! " which he
said that we might learn how infinitely more
than himself he loved the great God.   In the
same way, the force of his affection appears in
this other desire, that his bones might be so
many burning lamps, and his blood the purest
oil, in order that he, Augustine, might be
entirely consumed in the worship and service
of God.   This new idea demonstrates how
active and ready for sacrifice his love was.
Again, who has not heard that outburst of his
inflamed spirit, when speaking in the name of
every human heart, he proclaims : " Thou hast
made us for thyself, O Lord, and never can our
hearts find rest until they rest in Thee ! "   He
is usually represented with his own heart all
on fire, to signify his perfect charity.   Oh !
would that every daughter of St. Angela, his
spiritual child, walked before the face of God,
like this saint of " the burning heart" !

St. Francis de Sales, animated with a similar
desire, would often say to his dear daughters,
who also follow the rule of St. Augustine :
" All for love, my sisters."   Yes, the Spouse of

Jesus should accustom herself to do all for love. What love? The purest charity. If she prays let it be for the love of God, and not through fear of being penanced if she is negligent, or because her superior obliges her to pray, or in order not to lose an employment, or lest she should not be esteemed; and far less must she allow herself to be moved by any inordinate passion; but let God's love be the spring and the soul of all her thoughts, her desires, her words and actions; of the whole tenor of her religious life as becomes the true Spouse of Christ; and should it be appointed for her to suffer, let her accept of that also in the same spirit of love. Then will her holy state become truly a paradise on earth, and God in his merciful goodness will bless her with powerful helps for the perfect fulfilment of the other duties of her holy vocation, which, properly speaking, is no other than a vocation of divine love.

II.

AND THEN YOUR NEIGHBOUR.

The second commandment, says Jesus, is like to the first: *Thou shalt love thy neighbour as thyself.* [1] What an important exhortation especially for those who by their vocation are obliged to aim at Christian perfection, and who even as religious, have assembled for this end in a particular association. Moreover, the accomplishment of this commandment, as the Disciple of Charity assures us, is a certain mark that we keep the fundamental precept of the love of God, of which we have spoken, and is likewise an indispensable condition of its observance, for we read in the Epistles of St. John : *He that loveth not his brother whom he seeth, how can he love God whom he seeth not. And this commandment we have from God, that he who loveth God, love also his brother.* [2] Our Lord Jesus Christ expresses Himself still more clearly when He says : *By this shall all men know that you are my disciples, if you have love, one for another.* [3] So that the best mark that His spirit animates a community is not that they fast, pray and labour a great deal, but that they love one another, and that their charity exists in the fullest sense of the words

---

[1] St. Matt. xxii. 39.   [2] St. John, iv. 20, 21.
[3] St. John, xiii. 35.

of the commandment; that is, that each religious loves her sister as she loves herself. To excite this fraternal charity, the Spouse of the Saviour should often reflect that her religious sisters are likewise her natural sisters in Adam, our first father, and have become so in a far more intimate and exalted sense in Jesus Christ; that they are all created to the image of God, redeemed by the Blood of the Saviour, and that they have been chosen from amongst the children of men, and called to the religious state; that the Almighty lavishes on them innumerable graces, that He preserves them from many dangers, that He frequently nourishes them with His adorable Body and Blood, and finally, that they are all her companions on the road to eternal life. Let her also consider that there is no act of virtue whereby she can better prove her love of Jesus and Mary than by the exercise of the same charity, and none which so likens her to her Divine Spouse. *Love one another*, He says, *as I have loved you.*[1] Then, contemplating the Saviour giving Himself up to the death of the

---

[1] St. John, xiii. 34.

Cross through charity, let her reflect that her salvation is attached to her fulfilment of this precept. For even though you possessed all the other virtues that can sanctify a religious, if you have not fraternal charity, all the rest is but a vain show, an illusion of the evil spirit. Instead of being on the way to heaven, you are, with all your pretended virtues, in the road to perdition. The Sacred Text declares that one of the things the Lord hateth, *is one that soweth discord among brethren,*[1] and, as a consequence, among sisters of one and the same community ; and elsewhere we read that: *He that loveth not, abideth in death.*[2]

If we now turn to consider the marks of holy mutual charity, we find them in these words of St. Paul. *Charity,* he says (and here we are to understand all this of fraternal charity), *is patient, is kind : charity envieth not, dealeth not perversely : is not puffed up, is not ambitious, seeketh not her own, is not provoked to anger, thinketh no evil, rejoiceth not in iniquity, but rejoiceth with the truth : Beareth all things, believeth all things, hopeth all things, endureth all*

---

[1] Prov. vi. 19.   [2] 1 St. John, iii. 14.

things.[1] Let the Spouse of Christ examine and compare her conduct with these undoubted signs, that she may discover whether she abides in charity, possessing these marks of predestination.

Most certainly, we shall not find them in the impatient, fretful religious, who is unkind and unfeeling towards her sisters ; who envies them, tries to set herself above them ; who is puffed up with pride, though wearing the habit of humility; punctilious and fond of being distinguished ; always seeking herself and her own interests; easily offended, prone to judge. uncharitably, to suspect and to give out her rash judgments and suspicions ; who secretly rejoices at the defects of her sisters, and grudges them their advantages ; who is ever trying to assert her pretended rights, and neither believes in, nor hopes for, anything good of others. Assuredly such a person is a religious only in name and in externals, but not by any means so in spirit and in truth ; for her spirit is diametrically opposed to the charity of God, and therefore she can have no pretensions to the

[1] 1 Cor. xiii. 4, 5, 6, 7.

title of His Spouse. This self-worshipper
might, on the contrary, be likened to a nest of
hornets, so full is she of sins and imperfections;
or to a thorny bush, which you cannot touch
without being wounded; whilst a community
of true sisters in Jesus may well be compared
to the pure honey of heartfelt joy and consolation; their mutual charity excusing and veiling
each other's unavoidable defects, and so preventing the spiritual interests of the house from
sustaining any detriment.

We have still briefly to consider how this
precept of fraternal love is to be reduced to
practice. Our Lord's own explanation on the
subject concerns His Spouses equally with the
rest of mankind. He says: *All things therefore whatsoever you would that men should do to
you, do you also to them.*[1] And elsewhere:
*As you would that men should do to you, do
you also to them in like manner.*[2]

And the Holy Spirit speaking by Tobias says:
*See thou never do to another what thou wouldst
hate to have another do to thee.*[3] These sacred
words furnish us with an infallible rule of con-

---

[1] St. Matt. vii. 12.   [2] St. Luke, vi. 31.
[3] Tobias, iv. 16.

duct. All that you would wish your sister to do for you, do you the same for her; but what you would wish her to avoid in your regard, refrain from giving her to endure. This is a clear and comprehensive direction. Carry it out, and you will have accomplished the law of love, drawn down upon your soul the most abundant graces, and enriched it with every virtue. Occasions for exercising it will continually present themselves, but it is well to enter into details. You practise this divine charity as often as you pray for your sisters, begging of God to aid them with His grace, that they may faithfully keep their holy vows, their rules, and constitutions; and thus become *perfect*. Its lustre shines forth in the religious who sincerely rejoices in the spiritual progress of her sisters, who has the highest opinion of them all, and never utters a word contrary to the esteem she entertains for them; whose conduct towards all is marked by amiability and deference; and who, in short, proves that she loves them, being ever eager to render any service in her power, to supply for others, or to aid in whatever work may be most pressing. By this affectionate inclination to assist each other, all the hearts in a religious community become knit together in Jesus Christ.

The infirmary, as we may observe, presents a most favourable field for the exercise of this holy, active charity; and there should not be found a worldly home, in which the patient, though even a father or mother, was more kindly and devotedly cared than the religious by her sisters. These have far more to excite and fortify them in the discharge of difficult duties, and to inspire the soothing attentions so grateful to the sick, for they are acting by the spirit of Jesus; hence their motives become supernatural and divine, while those of seculars are natural, terrestrial, and human.

We come, in the last place, to a point of capital importance, which is that each one make manifest the strength of her charity by the sweetness, patience, and courage with which she tolerates the little weaknesses of her sisters; complying with the doctrine of St. Paul: *With all humility and mildness, with patience, supporting one another in charity ;*[1] and elsewhere: *Bear ye one another's burdens, and so you shall fulfil the law of Christ.*[2] This is an exhortation

---

[1] Eph. iv. 2.   [2] Gal vi. 2.

which religious cannot too often meditate; for, humanly speaking, it is impossible that in the society of so many persons there should not be found failings that must be borne with generously, unless we would have peace disturbed at every moment, and the monastery transformed from a paradise into a prison.

Even suppose all its inmates to live like saints, and to have no thought but of giving each other proofs of mutual love, and of advancing in perfection; God's providence would nevertheless permit, as a trial of patience and for the greater increase of merit, that they should still have to carry one another's burdens, owing to the great diversity of temperaments, views, and inclinations—sin, all the time, excluded.

This is a truth forgotten by some who, on entering a religious community, expect to meet none but angels, and take alarm if they come in contact with imperfections which they find disagreeable to endure. Vocations have even sometimes given way under the shock. But whoever reflects diligently will find that this providential arrangement, far from being injurious, affords the best opportunity for exercising that virtue which the

Apostle tells us, "*beareth all things ;* and with it, every other virtue that ought to adorn her who has taken up the Cross of her Saviour in the true spirit of self-abnegation.

If the love of Jesus be in us, it will support all with us. The enemy of our souls will then lose the power he is so ready to exert, of representing the slight imperfections that displease us in others, as matters of consequence ; and we shall be saved from imagining faults where they really do not exist; and also enabled to view those that are clearly obvious, with an indulgent charity which will render them quite supportable. Of such a community the Psalmist says : *Behold how good and how pleasant it is for brethren to dwell together in unity.*[1] The Holy Spirit compares it to the perfume that exhaled from the sacerdotal vestments of Aaron.

In fact, the Monastery wherein fraternal charity reigns after the manner we have described, is filled with the perfume of religious discipline, and of all virtues, to the great consolation of the community, and the very great

---

[1] Ps. cxxxii. 1.

edification of the faithful. The latter part of the foregoing remark is the more important, as we know how severely a convent is decried, when there is any pretext for suspecting its members of disunion. Calumny has almost always a share in such reports, at the instigation of the demon, who tries to rob God of His glory, and to hinder many souls from following their vocation. But it is not to be denied that they are sometimes, in a certain measure, true. Unfortunately there may not exist in all convents that complete harmony which would leave Satan and his ally, the world, unsupported by that shadow of truth which gained credit for these false statements.

It should, therefore, be the care of every religious to guard against the entrance of the spirit of discord, aversion, coldness, touchiness, &c. ; and, for the love of Jesus, to exercise charity with heroic courage, and invincible sweetness and patience. Ursulines should take this recommendation specially to heart. They are called to labour for the instruction of youth, whilst working out their own salvation, and consequently require a superabundant degree of charity. Without this their influence over the children whom they educate, will fail to be salutary.   But whoever is eminent in this divine science will be entitled to have applied to her these beautiful words of the Canticle of Canticles : *We will run after thee to the odour of thy ointments—young maidens have loved thee.*[1] That is, the young persons of whom she has the direction, attracted by the force of her charity, will imitate her example to their own great spiritual advantage and that of their neighbour ; and thus she will be blessed in her employment for the salvation of souls, and the greater glory of God.

CHAPTER II.

OF UNION AND MUTUAL CONFORMITY.

"Then follow those things which we have ordered to be observed in your monastery. As your great object in assembling together is to live in unanimity and concord, you should endeavour to have among you but one heart and one soul in God."

ACCORDING to the will and good pleasure of God, as well as to correspond with the design

[1] Cant. i. 3, 2.

St. Augustine had in instituting his holy Order, we ought to be able to say of every community professing his rule, what is said of the first Christians, that *they had but one heart and one soul.*[1]   The two conditions absolutely necessary for the accomplishment of this design, are the two virtues of which we have hitherto spoken : love of God, and love of the neighbour ; especially fraternal charity carried to a high degree of perfection.

Assuredly the community in which this two-fold charity reigns, will have but one heart and one soul, if we consider the sentiments of its members.   But in community life it is necessary that this union of minds should be manifested externally, and to this end Rules and Constitutions have been written.   From their observance spring that admirable discipline and union which justly amazes St. Basil, and which, to use the words of St. Paul, offers a spectacle to the angels of heaven.   For, is it not admirable to see persons of such various tempers, talents, and opinions, living together in that perfect harmony which forms the subject of our Divine

---

[1] Acts, iv. 32.

Lord's prayer: *I pray that they may be one, as Thou Father in Me, and I in Thee.*[1] And let us here remark that when Jesus appeared in the world, He immediately ordered the angels to announce peace to men of good will. It is peace that He recommends to His disciples in His discourse at the Last Supper: and "peace" is His salutation to them on the glorious day of His resurrection. This precious gift is essential for religious communities; and it is their portion according to this declaration of our Lord: *Where two or three are assembled in my name there am I in the midst of them.*[2]

The spirit of union and conformity here treated of, consists principally of the following points:

1. In union of minds by the bond of charity already dwelt upon at some length.
2. In union of religious discipline; that is, in the fervent and zealous resolution of every one in the community to observe silence, and all else that is prescribed or regulated for them, and to acquit themselves piously of the office and other prayers said in common.

[1] St. John, xvii. 21.   [2] St. Matt. xviii. 20.

3. In union of wills; all being determined to pursue with ardour the practice of the virtues that constitute Christian perfection, which is the end and object of the religious state, and at which, everyone called to this holy way of life, is strictly bound to aim.

All the religious in a community ought to endeavour to excite each other to aspire to this noble end, as did St. Bernard, who, writing to the brethren who dwelt amongst the Alps, says: "Let us persevere in the life we have embraced, preferring to be despised in the house of God rather than dwell in the tents of sinners. Now, our life is humility, voluntary poverty, obedience, peace, and joy in the Holy Ghost. It is our life to love fasting, watching, prayer, manual labour, and, above all, to walk in the perfect way of charity."

In the fourth place, this union consists in the preservation of interior and exterior peace. Yes, it is chiefly in religious houses that we should find our Lord's benediction realized: *My peace I leave you.*[1] And His Apostle tells those who abide in them : *To preserve the unity*

_____
[1] St. John, xiv. 27.

of the spirit in the bond of peace.[1] As to what concerns interior peace, the Spouse of Christ will strive to acquire it by purifying her conscience from every stain of voluntary sin, and by exercising herself in frequent acts and affections of Christian hope, with entire submission to the will of God, and unshaken confidence in His Divine Providence ; lastly, by her intimate relations with Jesus Christ in the interior life, walking always in His holy presence.

Thus the Spouse, faithfully observing those four points, will be filled with that peace which the Apostle wishes to all, and the sweetness of which, he says, surpasses all understanding. She will also preserve exterior peace with her sisters by her calmness, her mildness, her holy inward joy, and by the generous charity with which she endures their failings.

We shall now point out somewhat in detail how a religious might come to lose her interior and exterior peace, and so trouble the union of her community.

A person may lose interior peace by want of vigilance over herself, and by not being fully resolved to keep her tranquillity of mind, for-

[1] Ephes. iv. 3.

getting what the Royal Psalmist says: *Seek after peace, and pursue it.*[1] You fail against this highly important precept by not watching over your heart and imagination; and by allowing too much liberty to your senses. A curious religious will never enjoy interior peace—it is not peace that she *seeks after*, but rather disturbance and disquietude.

These are the objects of her pursuit when she permits her thoughts to be occupied about many things that concern her not, and only give rise to anxiety. It is the same when mind and heart become entangled in a multitude of affairs, which, if she had not the curiosity to meddle with them, would have left her in perfect repose, but which now painfully excite her feelings and affections.

She seeks trouble with her curious eyes, for she wishes to see, and does see, a variety of things, which, far from satisfying, cause her uneasiness. How unlike holy Job, who, though living in the world, had made a compact with his eyes[2] that they should not look on any object that might rob him of his peace of heart,

---

[1] Ps. xxxiii. 15.   [2] Job, xxxi. 1.

and how contrary to the wish of David when he
prayed : *Lord, turn away my eyes that they
may not see vanity.*[1]

She seeks trouble by her ears, when, impelled
by curiosity, she listens to what will bring nothing but trouble to her soul.   Much better
would it be for her, the Spouse of Jesus, to console herself, like holy David, by repeating : *To
my hearing, Lord, Thou wilt give joy and gladness,
and the bones that have been humbled shall rejoice.*[2]
Would it not be disgraceful if a religious community were found to be fonder of news than
are people in worldly society ?

The tongue of the inquisitive puts questions
on subjects, regarding which it were better for
her never to be informed.   The Holy Spirit
says: *In the abundance of words there shall not
want sin,*[3] and, we may add: there shall not
want vexation.   In the Book of Proverbs it is
written : *For the sins of the lips, ruin draweth
near to the evil man: but the just shall escape out
of distress.*[4]   And St. James says : *If any one
thinks himself to be religious, not bridling his tongue,*

---

[1] Ps. cxviii. 37.   [2] Ps. l. 10.   [3] Prov. x. 19.
[4] Prov. xii. 13.

but deceiving his own heart, that man's religion is vain.[1]

Finally, the feet of the curious bring them into difficulties, by bearing them to places where they can find only distractions and dissipation, as, for instance, when they are much in the parlour, or when, without permission, they are to be seen in places through the house, where, properly speaking, they have nothing either to do or to say.

Another foe to interior peace would be a mania for writing useless letters, and a desire to interfere in the concerns of seculars. Those who indulge such tendencies cannot enjoy repose, and may even militate against the tranquillity of their monastery.

As to exterior peace, it may be injured in the three following ways : First, by murmuring against the arrangements made by the Sisters in the principal offices, but, above all, by murmurs against Superiors. Wo to the house where the orders and wishes of Superiors are criticised, or where any ill feeling is manifested against those who are zealous to preserve religious discipline.

[1] St. James, i. 26.

Peace and union would be utterly ruined in this deplorable case.

Secondly : by aversions and dislikes among the Sisters themselves, the sad results of which would be rash judgment of each other's conduct, detraction, and tale bearing ; yet these strong words of the Holy Spirit ought not to be forgotten : *Hast thou heard a word against thy neighbour, let it die within thee, trusting that it will not burst thee.*[1] Where the contrary is practised, it is clear there can be no concord. Theologians teach that there is no way by which religious may sin mortally with so much facility as by detraction against each other, because, on one side, the honour of their brethren and sisters is something most exalted and delicate ; and, on the other, community life, placing them in perpetual contact, offers many occasions of wounding it.

In the third place, this precious and all-desirable peace is troubled by an evil quite opposed to the preceding, namely, particular friendships. Such intimacies never exist in a community without disturbing its harmony, for they con-

---

[1] Eccles. xix. 10.

tain within them a sort of injustice to other Sisters who are neglected ; this arouses jealousy, suspicions, melancholy, and envy, which are all destructive of peace, and their effects upon union and concord may be compared to the mischief done by moths in a wardrobe.

"The sickness of the mind," says St. Isidore, "eats into the heart, torments the body, and irritates the soul." And, would to God, that similar friendships did not give rise to the violation of the most important constitutions, nay, even of the vows. Another evil, also, is possible by a particular permission of God. The bond of this friendship, not founded on virtue, may be broken, and two, who were once fast friends, become irreconcilable enemies. St. Augustine has said : "As the best wine makes the best vinegar, so friendships like these often change to deep and bitter hatred." But they who reflect on the curse of God, which is recorded in Holy Writ, against those who bring dissension into a community, will make serious resolutions to avoid so great an evil, and will labour to their utmost to secure the blessings of concord. Happily, success is certain, if we take care to preserve ourselves from the faults

that have been mentioned, or to correct ourselves of them if they have been contracted,
using all possible means to maintain peace in
our own hearts, and then to extend it to others.
For this, mortification is necessary, especially
the mortification of our evil inclinations. Happy
is she, who, for love of holy peace, generously
mortifies her interior and exterior. She per-
forms a penance more meritorious than if she
fasted all her life, and in sackcloth and ashes.
The admirable instruction of St. Paul should
be also borne in mind: to *become all things to
all*[1] for the love of Jesus Christ; you will
gain a return of love, and, as the proverb says:

> " The peaceful prevail,
> When the quarrelsome fail,"

all will succeed according to your wishes, but,
of course, only in the measure that God pleases,
and that He sees is conducive to your salvation.

In the last place, we ought frequently and
fervently—in general, and in particular, pray
for this blessing—"Grant us peace in our days,

---

[1] 1 Cor. ix. 22.

O Lord, for there is none to fight for us and protect us but Thou, O Lord, our God!" We intercede so often for the repose of the souls in Purgatory, and desire for them the peace of God; let us do no less to obtain it for our living selves, and to ensure that the light of grace may perpetually shine upon us. If we do so earnestly and often, Jesus will enter by the closed door of the monastery, as He did formerly into the supper-room at Jerusalem, and will bestow His peace on the community. Yes; keep peace, says the Apostle St. Paul, *and the God of peace and charity will be with you.*[1]

II.

The words of the holy Rule already quoted, are a powerful exhortation to fervour in our state, and to the esteem and love of our vocation; they teach us to reflect often on the motives that led us to embrace religious life, and on the incomparable grace by which we were drawn thereto. Let us imagine that our glorious Father St. Augustine, speaking to the

[1] Phil. iv. 9.

heart of his daughters, addresses to each these touching words:—"Consider, my child, that God has withdrawn you from the house of your father, and from the tents and habitations of sinners, and inspired you to follow Him, with the generation of those who seek His face, and walk in the right way; that He has incorporated you in the virginal army of the lilies who dwell together in the same place, and are fed at the table of glorious poverty." By these words this holy father wishes to remind his children of the vocation which has called them from the tumult of the world, and the company of the wicked, to solitude, and to the society of fervent and generous souls, who are aspiring to virtue and perfection. It is true that every postulant who has a real vocation enters religion with this object in view; but unfortunately, some do not persevere to the end in their sentiments of gratitude for the grace of God. They grow accustomed to their happiness, and relax in the ardour which animated them when they crossed the threshold of their sacred asylum ; when, for the first time; they entered their cell ; when, for the first time, they saw themselves clothed in the holy

4

habit; when, finally, they were united to the
Spouse of virgins at the solemn moment of their
profession.   Oh! if the ardent zeal which then
filled their hearts had been preserved, how
easily and how quickly they would have ad-
vanced in the road to perfection; they would
have seen the grandeur of their vocation more
clearly every day, and would have made continual efforts to correspond with it.   Alas!
this tender and effective love cools but too
often; and instead of growing in holiness,
these faithless souls are meriting the complaint
and reproach of our Lord Jesus in the Apoca-
lypse :—*I have somewhat against thee because
thou hast left thy first charity.*[1]   And what will
result from this conduct?   Ah! our Lord
threatens :—*Do penance, and do the first works*
(remembering what thou hast been); *or else I
come to thee, and will move thy candlestick out
of its place.*[2]   Yes, God will give to souls more
faithful the graces destined for you; you will
fall into still greater obscurity and spiritual
dereliction; and even the time may come when
your holy vocation, far from furnishing an

[1] Apoc. ii. 4.   [2] Apoc. ii. 5.

assured hope of predestination, may be a subject of most terrible apprehensions, when you
reflect on these words from the first Epistle of
St. Peter :—*Judgment should begin at the house
of God.*[1]   And these equally impressive :—
*Unto whomsoever much is given, of him much
shall be required.*[2]

In order, then, not to transform into mortal
poison the consoling sweetness and invigorating
perfume of the remembrance of her holy vocation, the Spouse of Christ ought often to repeat
the words with which St. Bernard was wont to
animate himself to fulfil his duties perfectly :—
" Bernard, Bernard, why camest thou hither ?"
As if to say :—If it was to live after the
manner of worldlings, you ought to have stayed
in the world ; but since you have offered yourself in sacrifice to God, by your own solemn
act, you have contracted a strict obligation of
accomplishing fully what you swore at the foot of
the altar ; for it is written : " It is better not
to make vows, than, once made, not to keep
them."   Ponder on those words, and follow the
example of St. Bernard, and of all zealous and

[1] 1 St. Peter, iv. 17.   [2] St. Luke, xii. 48.

fervent religious. Ask yourself every day, or write on a slip of paper that you will often see, WHY CAMEST THOU HITHER? Perhaps it was to follow your own will, and live according to your pleasure. If so, it would have been better you remained in the world; but since your choice has been the religious life, and that you have vowed yourself to it, be fervent in the performance of your sacred contract, lest otherwise you may be numbered with the five foolish virgins of the Gospel, who, not having oil burning in their lamps, were refused admittance by the Bridegroom. Oh! how terrible were the words that resounded in their ears, when, knocking to be let in to the marriage, the answer came: I KNOW YOU NOT.[1]

May the Almighty in His mercy preserve all the members of this holy congregation from hearing that dread sentence! May He fill them with zeal and love for their vocation, and admit them, one day, with the wise and fervent virgins, to the nuptials of the Lamb. Amen.

[1] St. Matt. xxv. 12

CHAPTER III.

ON POVERTY.

"No one should possess anything as her own, but let all be in common. Food and clothing should be distributed to each religious by the Superior; not equally to all, for all have not the same necessity, but to every one according to her peculiar want; for so we read in the Acts of the Apostles : that *all things were in common* amongst the first Christians."[1]

THERE are two kinds of poverty. The first is that of the worldly poor, who do not possess means to procure even the necessaries of life. To them the Royal Prophet offers his consolation in the 9th Psalm: *And the Lord is become a refuge for the poor : a helper in due time in tribulation.*[2] The second kind of poverty is · that of the poor in spirit, who, for the love of Jesus Christ, abandon their possessions to live in voluntary poverty; that is, they renounce all property in order to please God more, and to possess Him more fully in that heavenly

---

[1] Acts, ii. 44.   [2] Ps. ix. 10.

kingdom, which our Lord's Gospel, in the out-
set, promises to the poor in spirit.

Our Divine Saviour's invitation is, indeed,
pressing. His promises are clear and magnificent. He says : *If thou wilt be perfect, go, sell
what thou hast, and give to the poor, and thou
shalt have treasure in heaven : and come follow
me.*[1] Again, speaking of his Apostles, and in
answer to St. Peter, who said : *Behold, we have
left all things and have followed thee; what, therefore, shall we have ?* Jesus replied : *You who have
followed me in the regeneration, when the Son of Man
shall sit on the seat of His majesty, you also shall
sit on twelve seats, judging the twelve tribes of
Israel.*[2] And in the touching Sermon on the
Mount : *Blessed are the poor in spirit : for theirs
is the Kingdom of Heaven.*[3]

Therefore, St. Bernard says : " If you want
to go to heaven, employ the infallible means,
and that is poverty." And, St. Thomas of
Aquin writes : "Poverty is our guide to heaven ;
she makes it easy for us to avoid sin and to
preserve virtue ; she procures for us true repose
of mind and heart ; rejoices us with spiritual

[1] St. Matt. xix. 21.   [2] St. Matt. xix. 27, 28.
[3] St. Matt. v. 3.

consolations; augments our merit, and secures our heavenly inheritance." But there can be no doubt that the poverty to which these precious advantages are attached as a prerogative, is that alone which is practised in accordance with the Gospel counsels, because it is only in this case that a man renounces with all his heart, through the virtue of poverty, all right to earthly things, in order to aspire to celestial goods with full liberty and fervour.

Seeing, then, that the hopes attached to this voluntary poverty raise us so powerfully heavenward, and that, on the other hand, we receive in religion all that is necessary for us, it is easy to understand that if we keep our vow faithfully, it is, and ought to be, accompanied by the effects enumerated by St. Thomas, and that it deserves to be termed the bulwark of our holy state; for, as poverty, observed in spirit and in truth, opens our hearts to the free entrance of supernatural favours, so negligence in the discharge of this essential vow, introduces the spirit of the world and soon brings on the total ruin of religious discipline.

Therefore, let every Spouse of Jesus, every one who loves her salvation, her vocation, and her holy Order, labour to keep this vow most perfectly, according to her rule and constitutions.

1st. By possessing absolutely nothing without the permission of her Superior.

2nd. By using the different objects given to her, not as if they were her own, but as the property of the House.

3rd. Let her beware of ever keeping about her person, or in her cell, money, or what would be value for money, or of asking permission to do so, unless in a case of great necessity; above all, let her never conceal in her cell as much as one farthing.

It is terrifying to read of the way in which the fathers of the desert acted towards those who transgressed their vow on this point. They did not even bury them in consecrated ground, but dug a grave in some odious place and threw in with their bodies the money found in their possession, while, at the same time, they pronounced these awful words: "May thy money perish with thee." And do we not read in holy Scripture how God Himself punished Ananias and Saphira by St. Peter's ministry? That unhappy couple, because they wished to keep back part of the price they had got for their goods and yet to pass for having laid it all at the feet of the apostles, were struck with instant death. But, a far more terrible example still, is to be met with in Holy Writ, and any religious tempted to make herself a proprietor should look in spirit at Judas. Oh! what a deplorable end for the disciple of Jesus Christ, suspended by a halter from the fatal tree! and what could have brought him to that? The Gospel answers: "*He was a thief;*" he appropriated what was given for the whole college of the apostles.

Theft is the name applied by the masters of the spiritual life to the violation of the vow of poverty. The name is correctly applied. What a disgrace if a Spouse of Jesus were to become a thief in the house of the Lord. Trifles, even without the sanction of obedience, might expose her, with time, to imminent danger of falling into a mortal sin and ending, like Judas, in final impenitence. Let each one, then, make her salvation sure by carefully examining in what state her conscience is with regard to holy poverty.

1. Has she got anything in her own possession, or in the keeping of others, without the
permission of her Superior? This is the first
degree in the observance of the vow, according
to the letter of the constitutions. To fail
against it is to incur the guilt of sin; and, is
it not amazing and affrighting, to find a soul,
after voluntarily renouncing, perhaps, great
worldly possessions, become the slave of trifles
in religion? If it seem to her hard to ask
permissions, she should consider that, according
to the doctrine of the holy Fathers, such humiliations have more value in the eyes of God
than the working of miracles, or spending days
and nights in prayer and the practice of all
austerities. Yet, this degree of poverty does
not suffice for the truly poor in spirit. The
true Spouse of Jesus must come to the second
degree. It consists not only in not having anything without leave; but, moreover, in rejecting all superfluities and never asking permission for such.

St. Teresa had the custom of carefully looking over matters in her little cell, to see if
there was anything that could be done without.
It is well for those who follow her example, or

who at least take as their models those members of the community who are the most faithful and zealous in the observance of holy poverty.

Finally, the third degree is that which a
religious has attained, who not only does not permit herself anything superfluous, but who likewise bears patiently the want of what is necessary; who is rejoiced to have opportunities of
practising holy poverty; but of course in conformity with the rules of pious and wise discretion.

Speaking on this matter, St. Bernard asks the
very reasonable question : To which class of
the poor do those claim to belong, who are unwilling to undergo even a privation, and who
fill the monastery with complaints if their wants
are not all supplied? We may be certain that
persons living in the world, even those who are
well off, must frequently dispense with what
would befit their rank, or seem essential to
their comfort.

The time of sickness may sometimes supply
religious with occasions for practising holy
poverty. Should this occur let us, as true
spouses of Jesus, show that we prize them.
There can be no greater happiness for us than
to have arrived at that state in which we would

rejoice and bless God for giving us to experience some little inconvenience with Jesus,
and for his sake, in order thus to become more
like the Beloved of our souls, who, being rich,
became poor for the love of us, and who will
bestow an ample measure of grace now, and of
heavenly joy hereafter, for the lightest suffering borne in His service.

All know the example of sublime perfection
given by St. Elizabeth of Hungary, when, after
the death of the Duke, her husband, having
been turned out of her palace to beg her bread,
and endure every kind of affront, she, with
holy joy at finding herself, at last, like Jesus,
her Saviour, went into a Church of the Fran-
ciscans, and asked them to entone the *Te Deum!*
And shall a religious venture to murmur at any
privation! Should she not rather exult with
joy, and thank God for permitting her to resemble the poor, abandoned Jesus?

It is related also of St. Teresa, that she and
her nuns recited the *Te Deum* in choir, when
there was not, in the convent, a morsel of bread
for the day. The angels in heaven could not
have sung a canticle more pleasing to the Lord,
and it is little wonder that they should be the

messengers sent with help for His faithful servants.

The love of Jesus, the desire of following His divine example as perfectly as possible, and the remembrance of His promises, excited the generosity of these fine souls, and of many who have been their faithful imitators. It will be so likewise with us, if we meditate often on the same motives, and give them entrance into our hearts; we shall be strengthened to follow the example of our Divine Lord, born, for love of us, poor, in a stable, and who died so poor on the cross; and then we shall not only practise holy poverty, but, as our Constitutions, say: *We shall love it as our Mother.*

II.

"Let those who had worldly wealth put it in the common stock. But they who had nothing in the world should not come to the monastery for the purpose of having that which elsewhere they could not have. Their infirmities should, however, be relieved, and all their wants supplied, though their poverty might have been so great when in the world, that they were destitute of even the necessaries of life.'

There are three things My soul hateth, says the Lord, in the Book of Ecclesiasticus; and among these the first is: *A poor man that is proud.*[1] Would to God that this passage of Scripture was inapplicable to any religious. But, unfortunately, the application has been but too often made, and might still be made in our own days.

"There are some," writes St. Jerome, "who, in the world, found it hard enough to procure rye bread to support nature, and who now, in religion, require loaves of wheaten flour. They were formerly accustomed to hunger; they have now become dainty and delicate."

Experience, indeed, has often proved that persons belonging to the poorer and lowlier grades, have, on being admitted into a convent, seemed to forget their former state, and even later, to become dissatisfied with what was given for their use, although in the world they could not have procured for themselves as good. We are far from saying that this is always the case; on the contrary, many religious there are who, from "the lowest ranks of the worldly poor," have entered the cloister with no other

---

[1] Eccles. xxv. 3.

view than to seek Jesus, and carry His blessed cross.

As to the vow of poverty, those without worldly wealth may make it as meritoriously as if they had large possessions to resign. St. Augustine explains this at some length in his commentary on the words of St. Peter to our Blessed Saviour. *Behold, Lord, we have left all things, and have followed thee : what, therefore, shall we have ?* [1] This holy Father of the Church makes the excellent remark that our Lord does not reproach St. Peter, or say to him : " You seem to forget how poor you were before you followed me." Or, " What great things then did you leave, that you should expect the whole world in recompense ? " Here is the explanation : " My dear brethren," says the holy Doctor, " whoever has sacrificed, not alone what he possessed, but, moreover, all that he could aspire to, and of which he might eventually become possessor, has sacrificed a great deal."

Nevertheless, they who, from actual poverty, have attained to the religious state, ought

[1] St. Matt. xix. 27

to reflect well on the particular gratitude due to their holy Order for many temporal benefits ; and should endeavour to become ornaments to it by the humility, regularity, and sanctity of their lives, instead of priding themselves on having been raised by the religious profession to an equality with those " whom in the world they would not have ventured to come near."

St. Bernard deplores the abuse opposed to this recommendation. It is a folly and an impiety, he says, for those whom no one thought anything of in the world, to seek for esteem in the cloister; and to aspire to honours in the very house of God, where honour and vain-glory ought to be trampled under foot.

Certainly, monastic life cannot profit them unto salvation, but must rather turn to their ruin, if the better food and clothing it assures to them be made a subject of foolish vanity ; whilst those who were always accustomed to the comforts of life study here to practise holy poverty, humility, and renunciation.

Let the former remember these words of the Lord, written in the Book of Sirach : *God hath*

abolished the memory of the proud, and hath pre-
served the memory of them that are humble in
mind.[1]

CHAPTER IV.

OF HUMILITY.

" They should not be puffed up, nor esteem themselves
the more, because instead of keeping their wealth to enjoy
it in the world they have given it for the support of the
community ; for every other kind of sin works in our bad
actions, whereas pride insinuates itself into our very best
actions, in order utterly to ruin them."

St. Jerome exhorts religious not to esteem
themselves, and especially not to prefer themselves to others, on account of their birth ;
because in the cloister it is to exalted virtue
and not to worldly rank that regard must be
had.

If persons of higher station seem entitled to
any greater consideration than others, it is
solely on account of the Christian magnanimity
with which they vanquished special difficulties

---

[1] Ecclus. x. 21.

in following their vocation. Such souls, however, should watch carefully, lest the remembrance of what they left might engender a temptation to pride and vanity, and lead them to exalt themselves above their sisters. No doubt it would be exceedingly absurd for one to boast in religion of what she had seemingly despised when in the world; or to take occasion from the apparent contempt with which she had then treated temporal things, to glorify herself under the religious habit, which is looked upon as the livery of humility. This would be to act like a person, who on meeting a poisonous plant, should dig it up, and transplant it into her garden. What is pleasing in the sight of God is the dignity of our immortal souls, His living images; and the nobility of our nature, as the brothers and sisters of Jesus Christ, the Son of God, and King of Glory, to which nobility virtue bears testimony by its lustre and beauty. "You ought not," writes St. Jerome, "prefer yourself to others, on account of your birth, or disesteem them for being of lowlier condition. In the religious state an edifying life is the sole title to distinction; it alone decides who is noble or ignoble."

Virgins of Jesus, permit me to present to you a bright example of true spiritual nobility in the Blessed Gertrude of Aldenberg. Her father was Landgrave of Hesse, her mother, St. Elizabeth, Princess Royal of Hungary; and yet, when at the age of twenty-one, she was made Superior of the Convent she had entered, she acted as if her origin were the lowliest. She undertook the most humiliating labours, and was distinguished from the other sisters only by the greater poverty of her clothing. Her favourite maxim was: "Whoever is the greatest, ought to make herself the humblest and the least."

What we have said of worldly position is also to be understood of riches. Whatever wealth a religious may have brought to the monastery, it can never give her a right to think better of herself than of others who brought smaller means, or none at all.

Where, indeed, would be the advantage for us of becoming voluntarily poor by the holy profession, if that exterior act were to render us rich and proud in spirit—proud even of poverty itself? Better in that case to have kept one's property, and remained in the world instead of coming to wound fraternal charity in a religious house, and to bring down one's soul to greater poverty than when it was the owner of worldly riches. Such a person could have nothing to look forward to from the promises of Jesus : *You who have left all for love of Me, shall be one day seated upon thrones ;* and again : *Thou shalt have a treasure in heaven.*[1] For, instead of exciting the complacency of the Lord, she draws down upon herself His wrath and vengeance.

St. Isidore inculcates a truth which we would all do well to study. He says that a man who has been converted from an evil life, requires to be greatly on his guard, lest he begin to pride himself on the virtues that he has acquired ; and by doing so, fall at last into a lower depth of iniquity than that from which he had been rescued. It is incredible with what facility this species of pride, vanity, or vain-glory, finds admission within convent walls ; and what mischief it is capable of effecting. As rust consumes iron, so vain-glory secretly corrodes the interior life of a religious, and spoils all her

[1] St. Luke, xviii. 22.

good works. The time will come when we shall
see this clearly, though the revelation may be
postponed to that last awful moment when the
voice of the Lord will be heard in the terrifying words : *Give an account of thy stewardship.*[1]
But, independent of other considerations, since
it is the common opinion of the Doctors of the
Church, that true and solid humility is the
foundation of all other virtues, how can a
spouse of Christ, obliged by her profession to
tend to perfection, neglect the study of this
indispensable humility, or be remiss in its practice ? It can be acquired by prayer, and by
strong, persevering efforts in exercising its
acts. It should be the frequent occupation of
the soul to reflect, on one side, on the injury
she does herself if she fails in solid humility ;
and on the other, on the blessings and graces
which accompany this virtue, especially in the
religious state.

This state is justly compared to a paradise.
And what was it that precipitated the chief of
the Angelic host, and with him the multitude
that fell from heaven ? It was pride. Pride,

---

[1] St. Luke, xvi. 2.

which, as St. Gregory observes, is peculiarly a mark of reprobation. Far be it then from the religious, whose conduct ought to exhibit the lovely signs of predestination; far be it from her, even for a moment, to bear the ominous badge of perdition!

On the other hand, the Holy Ghost declares that *God resists the proud and gives His grace to the humble.*[1] If, then, we wish to acquire many and great graces, and this all do desire who have sincerely consecrated themselves to God, our most earnest care should be to exercise ourselves continually in solid humility, and consequently in humiliation. This we never shall be able to do, if for any cause whatsoever, but especially for any human motives, we prefer ourselves to one or other of our sisters. Instead of doing so, each religious should take to herself the words of the Apostle St. Paul in his Epistle to the Romans: *In all honour preventing one another;*[2] that is, each rendering to the others those kind services and thoughtful attentions that denote preference and esteem; and manifesting the same by look, by word, by

---

[1] St. Pet. v. 5.　　　[2] Rom. xii. 10.

the manner in which she salutes on meeting her sisters ; in short, by the entire tenor of her conduct. If it happened that a religious, priding herself on some worldly advantage, refused to salute unless she were saluted first, it might well be asked, how can she be the Spouse of Jesus—*for, do not also the heathens this ?* [1]

Would to God that under these heads we had not even the most trifling matter wherewith to reproach ourselves ! This fervent exercise of mutual humility would contribute to the maintenance of discipline and concord, at the same time that it would promote the sanctification of each individual religious. Let us remember this saying of our Holy Father, St. Augustine ; it is full of truth and energy : " If you ask me what virtue is, I answer, it is humility; if you put the question again, I again reply, humility; and if you return a third time to the charge, I must still repeat, humility." Amen.

[1] St. Matt. v. 47.

CHAPTER V.

OF PRAYER.

"Apply to prayer and meditation at the hours, and in the place ordained," &c.

ALTHOUGH the principal end of the Ursuline Institute is the instruction of young girls, and not the leading of a contemplative life, yet they are equally obliged to have a great zeal for prayer; whether, because one is more bound to labour for one's own salvation than for that of the neighbour, or because religious can be more useful to the neighbour in proportion as they are more united to God by the faithful and fervent exercise of prayer. For this double reason a fixed time is assigned for the several devotions of each day, as the Office of the Blessed Virgin, Meditation and the pious practices in use in each monastery, according to the customs established for the various festivals and solemnities.

It is a sacred duty, and one strictly binding on the conscience of a Superior, to see that this

holy work of prayer and immediate communing
with God be faithfully accomplished by herself
and her community; and that no one omits it,
either wholly or partially, without a permission
grounded on weighty reasons. For, if zeal for
prayer and union with God by meditation be
wanting in a monastery, all that remains of the
religious life is but as a piece of mechanism, incapable of merit, without spirit or vitality, and which
can scarcely subsist without recourse to rigorous
measures. Whereas, in a community imbued
with the true spirit of prayer, and faithful to
its practice, the Spirit of God acts on each of
its members, and impels them all to run forward in the road of Christian perfection. For
it is in prayer that the heart becomes more and
more inflamed with the love of God; and where
that sacred love burns, there too will be found
the plenitude and accomplishment of the divine
law, together with strength and courage in the
combats, trials, and temptations that are to be
encountered in the life of the spirit. The consolations and the unction of the Paraclete abound
there in the midst of crosses and afflictions;
and everyone experiences the immediate succour
of the Almighty in her spiritual and corporal

necessities. Such is the teaching of Holy
Scripture in the words: *The continual prayer of
a just man availeth much.*[1] And our Blessed
Lord himself solemnly protests it: *Amen, Amen,
I say to you : if you ask the Father anything in
My Name He will give it to you.*[2] These words
refer particularly to prayer offered up in common, according to this express assurance of our
Saviour: *If two of you shall consent upon earth
concerning anything whatsoever they shall ask, it
shall be done to them by My Father who is in heaven. For where there are two or three gathered together in My Name, there am I in the midst of them.*[3]

Let us add that religious assembled in choir
for prayer, form a reflection and an image of
the celestial spirits, and of the blessed before
the throne of God in heaven. St. Augustine
expresses himself as follows, regarding prayer
said in the choir : " We have," he says, " in St.
Matthew (chap. xxvi.) the doctrine and commandments of Jesus Christ to chant psalms and
sing the praises of God, after the example of
our Divine Master and Model, who prayed thus
with His Apostles after they had eaten the

[1] St. James, v. 16.   [2] St. John, xvi. 23.
[3] St. Matt. xviii. 19, 20.

Paschal Lamb; for, although properly speaking, this is the office of the angels and of the blessed, who are continually praising the Lord ; yet it is likewise suitable for us, whose desires are in heaven, to do on earth what the angels do above."

We know, as a fact, how sweetly St. Felix of Valois was consoled by being an eye-witness of this truth. One night, the eve of the Assumption, as he was entering the church, he beheld Mary, the august Queen of Heaven, surrounded by angels in the habit of his Order, chanting on earth the praises of God, and reciting the Office of the Feast as ordained by the rubrics; and the saint, in a transport of joy, instantly united his voice with this enrapturing choir of celestial spirits. It is not given to us to see with our corporal eyes this union between the choirs of earth and heaven; but it undoubtedly takes place each time that a Community assembles in the church or oratory for prayer, since Jesus Christ Himself assures us : *Where two or three are gathered together in My Name, there am I in the midst of them.*[1] And where He, the King

---

[1] St. Matt. xviii. 20,

of Heaven is, there must His Court be. Oh! that all who meet to pray together thought each time of this truth, what devotion and recollection would result, especially when they pray in a church in presence of our Lord in the Blessed Sacrament!

Let each religious, then, resolve to pray with the greatest fervour, and to persevere in prayer, so as to lose none of the precious graces that God designs to bestow on her through the intercession of our Immaculate Lady, or of the angels and saints, when she unites herself to them in the ardour of her prayers. But above all, let every spouse of Christ, whether she pray in public or in private, be so attentive to what she is doing, that her prayer may be indeed, a *prayer* in spirit and in truth.

With this in view let her accustom herself during ordinary duties to prepare her heart by attention to the divine presence, silence, short ejaculations, and fidelity in renewing her act of pure intention. Then, before commencing a formal prayer or meditation, she should place herself in the presence of God, and imagine, especially if about to recite the Office in choir, that she is going to pray in the sight of the heavenly court, joined by the angels and saints, who will offer her petitions before the throne of the Most High. By the devout recital of the prayer before the Office, *Aperi, Domine, &c.*, she will comply with the advice of the Wise Man : *Before prayer prepare thy soul, and be not as a man that tempteth God.*[1] And when once engaged in the holy occupation, her care must be not to entertain voluntary distractions, whilst she ought to be speaking to God, and receiving His heavenly lights.

In this way souls acquire a habit of recollection and union with God, instead of likening themselves to King Ochozias. We read in the fourth book of Kings, that this prince being ill, instead of consulting the God of Israel, sent to consult the god of Accaron. The name of this idol was Beelzebub, which signifies "a god of flies."[2] And is it not "a god of flies" that a religious consults, who listens to wilful distractions, and who, though bodily kneeling or standing in choir, is all over the house in fancy; or perhaps, unheeding the walls of the cloister, she revisits that world she had re-

---

[1] Eccl. xviii. 23.   [2] 4 Kings, i. 2.

nounced. Far from honouring the Heavenly Spouse by that prayer, she, on the contrary, presses deeper into her suffering Saviour's head the cruel thorns of His bloody crown; for the Divine Redeemer vouchsafed to undergo that torture in particular to atone for idle thoughts indulged in prayer. But, were a religious, besides being interiorly distracted, to allow her negligence to become apparent, and a source of disturbance to others, that would indeed be *the abomination of desolation in the holy place,*[1] and such conduct would deeply and painfully wound the tender Heart of our Saviour.

Let all, therefore, make it their constant care to become penetrated with the true spirit of prayer, and to yield edification to one another in this important point.

Involuntary distractions, we know, are blameless, and may, moreover, be improved into occasions for fresh victories and new merits. If we do what is in our power to repress them, God may even, in time, and as a recompense, deliver us altogether from voluntary distractions—an exemption with which He was pleased

---

[1] St. Matt. xxiv. 15.

to favour St. Aloysius, who was raised to the
prayer of quiet, in return for the courageous
perseverance with which he opposed all that
could divert his mind from God.

Religious should also animate their prayer
with filial confidence, and the most lively faith ;
and this above all, when it is a prayer of im-
petration, abandoning themselves perfectly to
the Divine Will for the accomplishment of the
petition, remembering these words of our Lord in
the garden : *Father, not My will, but Thine be
done.*[1] As to zeal and eagerness for prayer, we
have our Blessed Master's recommendations :
Always to pray, and never to faint ;[2] that is, to
keep our hearts united to God by piety and
love, even when we are not in the actual exercise of prayer ; and at the times that we may
enjoy uninterrupted converse with Him, to try
to establish our hearts more and more firmly in
this divine union.

Jesus has confirmed His doctrine by numberless examples. What a life of recollection and
prayer during the first thirty years of His
mortal existence! And what fervent petitions

---

[1] St. Luke, xxii. 42.   [2] St. Luke, xviii. 1.

His Sacred Heart was ever sending up to His
Eternal Father for the salvation of the world!
Then, before entering on His public life, He
sought a solitude still more profound, and
prayed for forty days in the desert. And after
He had surrounded Himself with disciples, He
frequently left them to spend whole nights in
watching and prayer. Finally, in preparation
for His bitter Passion, He prayed in the Garden
of Olives, and persevered for hours, notwithstanding His agony and bloody sweat.

Let us, with grateful love, imitate Him.
Could there possibly be a sweeter or more consoling employment for His true spouse than
that which opens the way into the life *hidden
with Christ in God.*[1] Wanting this interior life
of union, she would be a spouse only in name.

The crowning grace of perseverance is
attached to prayer. No one has ever failed in
her vocation who was fervent and faithful in
the discharge of this duty; particularly in that
branch of it which we call meditation, as this is
the means of obtaining the graces necessary for
overcoming tepidity and sloth, with His blessing on our efforts in His holy service. Those

[1] Col. iii. 3.

who neglect prayer, grow negligent likewise in all that is requisite for sanctifying them in their vocation. Hence, Blessed Albertus Magnus often said that prayer was more agreeable to God than fasting on bread and water, or disciplining oneself to blood.

O Religious Soul! you who truly love and esteem your sublime vocation, you who desire to save your soul, and to become more pleasing in the eyes of God, labour constantly to preserve and increase the spirit of prayer. Meditate often on the sufferings and death of our Lord, and on the eternal truths; and very fervently beg of God to grant you the precious gift of prayer, for with it you shall have all blessings.

II.

"Let no person perform any action whatever in the Oratory or Choir, but that for which it is destined, and which its name imports. And if even besides the prescribed hours, some, having leisure, wish to pray there, let those who have any other duty to fulfil there, not give cause of hindrance or distraction."

The place whereon thou standest is holy ground,[1]

[1] Exod. iii. 5.

said God to Moses. Every religious should imagine when entering choir that she hears these words. Here truly, is a holy place that has been consecrated to the service of God by special benediction. *Lord*, exclaimed Solomon, *O Lord, my God : hear the hymn and the prayer which thy servant prayeth before thee this day : that thy eyes may be open upon this house night and day : upon the house of which thou hast said : My name shall be there . . . . That thou mayest hearken to the prayer of thy servant and of thy people Israel, whatsoever they shall pray for in this place, and hear them in the place of thy dwelling in heaven ; and when thou hearest, shew them mercy.*[1] Graces attended with a special benediction are particularly attached to the sacred edifices in which God receives solemn worship under the New Law. They are also sanctified by the holy relics deposited in them ; but above all by the presence of Jesus in the Adorable Sacrament. Multitudes of the heavenly host are prostrate there before Him. And besides all this, how venerable to the religious soul must be a spot where she knows

[1] 3 Kings, viii. 28, 29, 30.

God is wont to grant graces to her sisters, and where she, herself, has received from Him innumerable favours in proportion as her conduct has corresponded with the sanctity of such holy ground.

St. Gregory, therefore, justly exhorts us not to permit anything unseemly in a place where the praises of God are chanted; His doctrine explained; and His blessings showered down in profusion.

Cardinal Hugo, enumerating some of the abuses which lead to the ruin of monasteries, commences with a negligent superior, a disobedient subject, a slothful junior, a self-willed ancient; and having pointed out other faulty characters, such as the curious, whose time is lost in reading or hearing worldly news; the tepid, who meddle in secular affairs; the quarrelsome, the vain, and the sister who is too nice about food, he ends with one who is irreverent in presence of the most holy sacrament.

Not alone when prayers are being offered up there in common, but at all times, the utmost respect should be observed in choir. Our Holy Father expressly desires that there should be nothing to disturb those, who, through private devotion, wish to pray there; and superiors are strictly obliged to ensure this.

Prayer, belonging to the essential exercises, and being ordained by the Constitutions of most orders, it is incumbent on every religious to avoid all that could interfere with exterior or interior devotion in the place specially consecrated to it. Those who are inattentive at their prayers, and who even interrupt them to speak without necessity, have but too much cause to apply to themselves the words of St. John Chrysostom: "One who speaks to an earthly king, speaks on subjects that the sovereign wishes to hear about, and on which he questions him. Were the inferior to break off the discourse, and introduce some matter foreign to it, it may easily be supposed that he would be made to feel that he had transgressed. Now you, when you pray, are speaking to the King of kings, before whom the angels tremble with respect. If you interrupt the conversation to speak of mud, and dust, and cobwebs, for the affairs of this world are no better in His eyes, how can you hope to escape His wrath" St. Bernard speaks to the same effect.

"It would be better," he says, "for those who recite the Divine Office to be altogether silent, for it is written: *Cursed be he who doth the work of God negligently.*[1] Such prayer would not *ascend as incense in the sight of God;*[2] but as a horrid stench, emanating from evil thoughts and criminal irreverences."

There have been holy persons present on occasions when the office was chanted indevoutly who, instead of hearing a sort of angelic concert, had their ears assailed with frightful howlings. *The prayer of the sinner*, says the Sacred Text, *is not pleasing to God.*[3] St. Romuald often declared that a single psalm, or a *Pater* and *Ave*, said with recollection, was worth more than a hundred recited with distractions. It is principally to those who are inattentive during devout exercises practised in common, that the well-known sentence may be applied: "He whose mind and heart are elsewhere, although present in body, is to be considered as absent." The enemy of souls leaves nothing undone to bring about this result with many; and when the signal is given to call the

Jer. xlviii. 10.   [2] Ps. cxl. 2.   [3] Prov. xxviii. 9.

religious to choir, his infernal troops prepare to disturb and distract them, while praising the Lord. Let all, therefore, be resolute in opposing the tempter, and by thus preserving their recollection of spirit, their own experience will make them exclaim with Jacob: *This is no other than the house of God, and the gate of heaven;*[1] and let the prayer of all arise to heaven with such force and might, that it may be granted to them to say with David: *We have received thy mercy, O God, in the midst of thy Temple;*[2] and also to find the words of our Lord verified: *Where two or three are assembled in My name, there am I in the midst of them.*[3]

We shall here add a remark on a complaint very frequently made. Some souls are so tormented, as they say, with dryness and aridity in prayer, whether praying in company with their sisters, or in private, that they consider it impossible for them to derive any fruit from this holy exercise. In order to give a suitable answer to this complaint, it is necessary first to know whence the aridity or dryness of mind proceeds.

[1] Gen. xxviii. 17.   [2] Ps. xlvii. 10.   [3] St. Matt. xviii. 20

It has three principal sources. First the state of one's health; for in the Book of Wisdom it is written that : *the corruptible body is a load upon the soul.*[1] Secondly, our faults; and then it is a punishment from God, when the soul by her imperfections and sins, especially her irreverence, has become unworthy of an intimate and familiar communication with Him ; finally, it may be a trial by the divine permission, for the purpose of strengthening the soul in humility and love of the Cross, thereby to introduce her to that life of faith, that will lead, later on, to a high degree of prayer. For it may be held as certain, that no one can attain to such a degree unless God has prepared her by great spiritual trials, which alone teach the soul to walk in true and solid humility, and to abandon herself entirely with confiding faith into the hands of God.

When God is pleased to subject a soul to this severe trial, without any fault of hers, she should, instead of indulging sadness or discouragement, endeavour to follow the example of St. Bernard. Whenever he was visited with

[1] Wis. ix. 15

this interior dereliction, he used to exclaim: " As often, my God, as you depart from me, I will entreat again and again, until I bring you back; never shall I cease importuning until you return, and grant me anew the joy of your presence." And not in vain shall we thus cry to the Lord; for if we have borne the trial with humility and patience it will be our sweet consolation to experience what the Prophet expresses in these words :

Thou didst turn away thy face from me, and I became troubled . . . . But the Lord hath heard, and hath had mercy on me, the Lord became my helper. Thou hast turned for me my mourning into joy : Thou hast cut my sack-cloth, and compassed me with gladness. To the end that my glory may sing to Thee, and I may not regret, O Lord, my God, I will give praise to Thee for ever.[1]

Ps. xxix. 8, 11, 12, 13.

III.

" When you are occupied in the service of the Church chanting the Psalms and Hymns, your heart ought to attend to what your voice pronounces, and chant only what you read should be chanted ; and what is not desired to be chanted you should not chant."

Some religious consider it a very hard and painful thing not to understand what they pronounce when reciting the Divine office. But can they not reflect that by this holy exercise the Church praises and blesses God by their lips ? And what a great and peculiar consolation should it not be for the Spouse of Jesus to know that the Almighty has chosen her out of an infinite number of souls, to pay Him this tribute of homage in the name of the Church. Moreover, if she possesses the spirit of prayer, and that she has exercised herself in meditation, she will find it easy during the recital of the office to intermingle affections of faith, hope, love, gratitude, &c., and to think of God and the things that appertain to Him. Add to this the infinite merit of holy obedience. According to the unanimous teaching of the Doctors of the Church, it is more meritorious to pick

up straws through obedience, than to apply to
the highest contemplation at the promptings of
self will.

One day that Blessed Jordan was asked if the
prayers that religious recite without compre-
hending them were pleasing to God, he answered : As a diamond in the possession of a
man who knows not its worth, is still as much a
diamond as if it were in the hands of an experienced lapidary, so the words of the divine
office uttered by those who do not understand
them, retain all their value before God, when
recited as a duty.   And as a petition presented
to a king, by one ignorant of its meaning, is,
nevertheless, received by the monarch as if that
person herself had composed it; even so, God, the
King of kings, accepts the prayer of those who
are unacquainted with the sense of the words
they pronounce, provided they say them with
devotion; as it is written : *Out of the mouths
of infants and of sucklings thou hast perfected
praise.*' A religious complaining one day to
the holy Abbot Pastor, that, although praying
always, he never felt his heart touched, in con-

' Ps. viii. 3.

sequence of not understanding the words; the Abbot answered : You ought not, on that account, cease to pray. Snake-charmers, by using a language, the meaning of which is unknown to them, force those reptiles to obey them; and in like manner, though we may be ignorant of the signification of the psalms and hymns that we recite, the evil spirits, those infernal serpents, understand them, and are put to flight. Therefore, let all the religious take pains to pronounce, clearly, fully, and with great devotion, every part of the office, in union with the will and intentions of the Holy Church, carefully rejecting every idle thought, and they may be certain that their prayer will please God, and be most salutary to themselves. St. Bernard often exhorted his monks in these terms : "I conjure you, my beloved, to join in the praises of the Lord, purely and generously." Generously, that is, not only with respect, but also with joy; not heavily or sleepily, yawning or giving out but a little thread of voice, abridging or omitting words, and thus disfiguring the work of the Holy Spirit.

When reciting the psalms, think what sublime sentiments they contain, or else, think of

God, of the mysteries of the life, passion, and death of our Lord; think of his Blessed Mother; exercise acts of the three theological virtues, or let your heart produce similar effusions. It is very useful to foresee and provide different intentions and reflections for the various parts of the office, as a means of exciting pious affections more readily, and of avoiding distractions.

For instance, at each *Gloria Patri*, one might purpose to renew her act of pure intention, and to adore the Most Holy Trinity in union with the whole celestial court. How many sublime acts of virtue may not a religious perform, who is faithful to this single practice ; what a tribute of lofty praise and ardent gratitude will she not have rendered to the Lord in the course of a year ! And how much greater still her merit will be, if she accompany the other portions of the office with similar acts of virtue, accustoming herself, for example, to recite acts of Faith, Hope, and Charity, Contrition, Reparation, Adoration, &c., at the Invitatory, the hymns, psalms, and lessons of Matins ; or to recite a psalm or hymn with the intention of obtaining some virtue, or of gaining the victory over a

particular fault. She may also imagine that
she prays with some choir of angels or saints;
with her Angel Guardian, her holy patrons, St.
Augustine, St. Angela, St. Ursula, &c.; with
the choir of holy virgins; with the Martyrs,
Confessors or Apostles; with Mary—nay, even
with Jesus Himself.

Having such thoughts and intentions, her
prayer will be replete with fervour and
devotion; her distractions being probably
fewer than if she understood the psalms and
hymns.

There is yet another abuse to be guarded
against in chanting the Office. It is due to
worldly-minded religious who try to pervert
the worship of God to the gratification of
their own vanity, employing that voice which
is His gift, in a spirit opposed to the will of the
Giver. Undoubtedly, it is good and laudable
to sing or chant in a full and fervent tone, but
to be proud of one's voice, or to make it a cause
for preferring self to others, is no less certainly
an evil. There are persons, who, considering
their voice something very precious, are careful to spare it during the ordinary psalmody,
but when they have to sing alone, or with but

one companion, they display all the power of their organs, to show how far they surpass others, perhaps also, to please creatures. A sister who chants fervently and humbly, though her voice be somewhat discordant, gives more glory to God, and more joy to His heavenly court, than one whose voice of perfect harmony, entones the divine praises only from a despicable motive of vain-glory. Does not the Apostle St. Paul expressly exhort us *not to walk in malice and envy, but to do all our works in charity?*

It is needless to say that the chant and music employed in the divine office are much to be esteemed, as it is most just to consecrate to the service of God everything capable of elevating the soul to Him. In the Holy Scriptures we find some striking examples. When the people of Israel were miraculously delivered from Pharao, Mary, the sister of Moses, with all the choir of virgins, sang a canticle of thanksgiving, in which they were joined by Moses, Aaron, and the people. We read also of David that he was very zealous in singing the praises of God, and that he composed a great number of psalms for the divine service in the Temple, and in them he mentions the solemn sound of instruments forming an accompaniment. The great and pious kings of Israel, Solomon, Ezechias, Josaphat, and Josias, followed this example. They were careful that the praises of God should be often celebrated in this manner in the Temple.

At the conclusion of the office we should say the *Sacrosanctæ*, with sentiments of sorrow, in order to obtain the remission of our faults of frailty in its recital, granted by Pope Leo X. to those who devoutly say this prayer.

With the consoling doctrine of St. John Chrysostom we shall end this chapter. "Consider," says this great saint, "what a happiness and what an honour you have enjoyed. You have been permitted to enter into intimate familiarity with God, to converse with Jesus Christ, to desire what you would, and to be able to exact all that you wished for."

No human tongue could declare the greatness of the dignity to which we are raised by this commerce with God, or the immense benefits that we derive from it; it is the means by which the heart of man attains to true nobility, learns to despise all earthly things, to rise above

them, and gradually to be united with, and in
a manner transformed into God Himself, so as to
become altogether spiritual and holy.

CHAPTER VI.

OF FASTING AND REFECTION.

"Overcome your flesh by fasting and abstinence in eating and drinking, inasmuch as your health will permit.
When a person cannot fast she should not take anything
out of the hours ordained for meals, unless when she is sick."

A Spouse of Jesus Christ having made a solemn
vow of chastity and angelical purity, is thereby
strictly obliged to employ all the means necessary for the preservation of this divine virtue.
One of the principal of these means is temperance in eating and drinking, as St. Chrysostom
remarks; declaring, "that temperance, and
reiterated fasts are the two bases of purity of
heart; and where these pillars are wanting,
virtue cannot subsist. It is certain that whoever imagines it possible to conquer the motions
of concupiscence, amidst abundance in eating
and drinking, is like one who would hope to

extinguish a fire by throwing in wood." St. Augustine says on this subject: " Fasting purifies the soul, subjects the flesh to the spirit, produces contrition and humility, banishes the illusions of the spirit of darkness, extinguishes the flames of impurity, and makes the pure light of chastity shine." According to the teaching of St. Cyprian, our sensual appetites are weakened by fasting, their sting is blunted, and the virtues that spring from pure, heavenly piety are planted in the soul, where they multiply and are preserved. St. Leo, Pope, writes, " From mortification and abstinence arise chaste thoughts and salutary consolations; the flesh dies to concupiscence, the spirit is fortified in virtue, and devotion is powerfully augmented." In the Book of Tobias it is said: *Prayer is good, with fasting and alms.*[1] In the Prophet Joel the Lord Himself exhorts us by these words: *Be converted to me with all your heart, in fasting, &c.*[2] In his Second Epistle to the Corinthians, St. Paul addressing all Christians, speaks thus: *Let us exhibit ourselves as the servants of God in much patience . . . . in fastings, in chastity. . . . .*[3]

[1] Tob. xii. 8.   [2] Joel, ii. 12.   [3] 2 Cor. vi. 4, 5, 6.

There are two kinds of fast to be distinguished : At certain times, and on fixed days, there is the ecclesiastical fast ; and besides this there is the fast prescribed by their Rule for different religious orders. All Christians are obliged to the former by the general law of the Church ; religious alone are bound to observe the latter, according to their rules and constitutions. Let Superiors be very careful not to contribute by over condescension to the decay of religious discipline on this point ; they should yield only when the health of individuals requires some indulgence by the advice of the physician, and with the consent of the confessor. St. Bernard, quoting the words of the Apostle, says, that "power has been given to Superiors, not for the destruction, but for the preservation of discipline." If, in this matter, discipline grow weak, a powerful wall of defence for angelic purity may be said to crumble away ; for St. Ambrose declares, that "Hunger is a friend to virginity, and an enemy to impurity." Satiety in food causes the loss of chastity, and nourishes evil desires and corrupt inclinations.

However, this abstinence should be accompanied by holy discretion ; that is, a degree of moderation is to be observed, that will prevent the body from being excited by too much nourishment, or enfeebled by too little. We learn this from St. Fulgentius, the disciple of the great St. Augustine. "God," he says, "would not be pleased with an abstinence that should render us incapable of reciting the divine office, or fulfilling the other duties of our state." Miracles have, from time to time, confirmed this truth. We read in the life of one of the saints, the holy Bishop Isfred, that God changed water into wine for His servant, who was unwilling to refresh himself with a salutary draught.

St. Jerome, too, recommends moderation in fasting, particularly for those who, when the fast is at an end, are apt to go beyond the bounds of temperance. He prefers exact and constant moderation to a fast thus interrupted by excess. In order that a religious may act securely in this matter, she should undertake absolutely nothing but by the advice and permission of her Superior and Confessor, remembering that the best penance for her is to follow the common life in all, and without exception; that is, to take food or other refreshment only when the community do so. This is the greatest and most meritorious mortification. All know, that even in mortifying herself, a religious might sin by obstinately preferring her own will to that of her Superior; and this is another case in which God has vouchsafed to shew by miracle, how much it displeases Him.

As to the sick and weakly, they should be specially cautioned against too much rigour. Superiors ought to use all possible discretion in their regard, acting towards them as kind and prudent mothers, and granting them the necessary dispensations, so that they may not break down before their time, but preserve their strength for the service of God. Making every allowance for this just solicitude and real charity for invalids, it is to be observed that nothing so readily brings a community into contempt as excess in eating and drinking. The aim and end of every religious order is, doubtless, to assimilate its members to the blessed in heaven, by victory over all their passions, and especially over the inordinate cravings of appetite. "Gluttony," says a holy Father, "was the cause of our losing Paradise; it is for abstinence to re-open the entrance."

It is very remarkable, and at the same time a salutary warning for us, to find what the Holy Scriptures say of the apostasy of the Israelites. It commenced in the midst of joyful festivities : *And they were eating and drinking.*

In like manner, it may unhappily be re-marked of any religious house where such feasting is the order of the day, that, besides its being possibly a cause of sin, it is also a sign that that community which God had called out of Egypt by many signs and wonders of His grace, has degenerated and returned to the idols which the world adores.

We meet in the Book of Job a very remark-able example on this subject. *There was a man,* says the Sacred Text, *in the land of Hus, whose name was Job. . . . . And there were born to him seven sons and three daughters. And his sons went and made a feast, and called their three sisters to eat and drink with them. And when the days of their feasting were gone about. . . . Job, rising early, offered holocausts for every one of them. For he said : Lest, perhaps, my sons have sinned.*[1]

And yet Satan obtained absolute power over

[1] Job, i. 1, 2, 4, 5.

them, and raised a violent tempest, which threw
down the house they were in, so that they were
buried alive. Is it not also written in the
Prophet Ezechiel: *Behold this was the iniquity
of Sodom, thy sister; pride, fulness of bread,
idleness . . . . And I took them away as
thou hast seen.*[1] Can anything be more shame-
ful than that a Community should resemble
Sodom and Gomorrha, whilst it ought to be a
reflection of the heavenly Jerusalem, of which
it is written: *The Kingdom of God is not meat
and drink.*[2]

Thus, as it is praiseworthy in a Superior to
provide charitably for the wants of her Community, so is it binding on her conscience to see
that no excess be introduced in the way of
nourishment; chiefly, because intemperance is
the mother of so many vices, and is incom-
patible with heavenly purity. St. John
Chrysostom confirms this truth by the following
severe sentence: "Even as chastity, if not
associated with fasting and temperance, is unable to subsist, and that it totters and tends to
its fall; so, on the contrary, if strengthened

---

[1] Ezech. xvi. 49, 50.   [2] Rom. xiv. 17.

and supported by those two pillars, it easily conquers and triumphs." Let us then be courageous, and overcome ourselves generously, remembering these words of our Lord: *The Kingdom of Heaven suffers violence.*[1] Let us not say that it is impossible for us—for when there is question of health and temporal life, are we not ready for the most frightful mortifications? If, for example, gangrene attack one of our limbs, are we not prepared to lose the diseased member in order to save life? And, is it possible that where eternal salvation is at stake, we should not do violence to our nature and conquer it, when our Lord Himself so pressingly exhorts us, saying: *Take heed to yourselves lest your hearts be overcharged with surfeiting.*[2] And elsewhere He says: *Unless you do penance you shall all likewise perish.*[3]

II.

"When you come to table, and all the time until you leave it, listen in peace and without any noise to the lecture that is made according to custom; to the end that not the mouth alone should receive its food, but that the ear may be nourished with the word of God."

Solomon says: *The just man eateth and filleth*

[1] St. Matt. xi. 12. [2] St. Luke, xxi. 34. [3] St. Luke, xiii. 3,

his soul.[1] How is an effect apparently so
singular to be explained? In this way; he
takes his food with a right intention, in due
measure, and in a proper manner; in other
words, he eats, not to content nature and sensu-
ality, but to accomplish the all-wise and all-holy
Will of God, who is pleased by that means to
preserve our life, and to give us occasions of
meriting, by the pure intention and fitting
temperance with which we fulfil His law.
For this reason, souls desirous of perfection
have always kept their minds more occupied
with spiritual things when at meals, than attentive to the food they were taking; hence the
custom in all fervent and regular communities
of having a spiritual lecture during repasts.
St. Augustine, even when Bishop, always had
pious reading at table. And if, as it sometimes
happened, speaking was permitted, the guests
were reminded to control the tongue, and consequently all their passions, by an inscription
couched in such terms as the following:

" Who of his neighbour loves to speak amiss,
Should know this table him forbidden is."

[1] Prov. xiii. 25.

St. Germanus, Bishop of Paris, also wished to have a spiritual lecture read during meals, that the mind might be refreshed at the same time as the body. St. Antoninus, Bishop of Florence, followed the same custom, and was so attentive to the lecture, that he observed and corrected the slightest faults of the reader. Even seculars have adopted this excellent practice to the very great profit of their souls. Charlemagne usually had the writings of St. Augustine read to him while he took his repast.

Superiors, therefore, should be strictly exact in not allowing the spiritual lecture during meals to be ever omitted. Fidelity to this observance is of more importance than can be thought, and in case any negligence had crept in, it should be effectually remedied. True religious will be always zealous for this point of their Constitutions, and will contribute as far as lies in their power to maintain it in full vigour. To consider this observance irksome, or to lead in any way to its being less valued, would indicate a tepid and worldly spirit. By this spiritual lecture it is that the repasts of religious may be distinguished from those of seculars. It testifies for them that if they still live in the flesh, at least that they do not live according to the flesh, but according to the spirit. Another advantage that it has, and one experienced by many, is that it renovates the soul, and is accompanied by precious inspirations from the Holy Spirit, especially when listened to with pious attention, and a great desire of deriving profit. Wherefore, both those who are at table, and those who serve, ought to be extremely careful to avoid the least noise. The repasts of religious are rendered truly spiritual and edifying by means of these precautions. It is right then that each of them should endeavour to discharge her duty perfectly in this matter; and if it happen that anyone have contracted a bad habit, let her correct it by means of the particular examen, that thus reformed, she may no longer give bad example to her sisters.

By acting in this way, whilst the body is being nourished, the soul will receive an aliment no less fortifying, as it is written : *Not in bread alone doth man live, but in every word that proceedeth from the mouth of God.*[1]

---

[1] St. Matt. iv. 4.

III.

"If the infirm, and those who have been delicately brought up, are treated differently from others in some little points, that should not displease nor seem unjust to the others, whose habits of life have contributed to their strength ; nor should these latter think the infirm happier because certain food is given to them which is not given to all ; but let them rather be consoled at possessing that health, of which others are deprived. . . . . . Let those esteem themselves the richest who have most strength to support frugality—for it is better to require little, than to have much."

Wo to you that call good evil,[1] says the Prophet Isaias. This malediction falls principally upon those who are grieved, and think themselves in a manner wronged, when, on account of ill health, one of their sisters gets something particular in the way of food, or other conveniences of life. Envy of that nature betrays a great imperfection, a great tendency to evil, and very little love of God and our neighbour. A Spouse of Jesus, whose sole desire should be to follow her Crucified Spouse in His humiliations, contempt, and sufferings, ought to rejoice if, by a

---

[1] Isaias, v. 20.

special permission of God, it happened that what was necessary were wanting to her for a time. This being so, how can she envy her sisters for being treated as their infirmities require.

We have a proof of the displeasure with which our Lord views even the shadow of envy, in the reply He made to St. Peter. A report that the Beloved Disciple should not die had spread about among the Apostles—Peter seems to have been a little jealous, and he curiously asked Jesus : *Lord, and what shall this man do ?*[1] Jesus contented Himself with answering him shortly : *What is it to thee ? Follow thou me.*[2] It would indeed be a very sad thing, and very deplorable, if, in a religious house, Superiors and sisters were exposed to rash judgments on this subject, and that vexation and envy crept in. What could the consequences be but discord, murmuring, uncharitableness, and grave dangers for salvation? And as the enemy of our souls knows well the evil done to a community when he can break the link of fraternal charity, he uses every stratagem to gain this

fatal end, and then profits by the opportunity
to try the power of his most violent temptations. Let every one guard against this snare
of the demon, and live in her monastery animated with the holy desire that all her sisters
should have the best as their due, and that her
own position might be conformity with Jesus,
suffering and neglected. Let each try to give
her sisters the preference in her heart; this will
effectually stifle all thoughts of envy.

On the other hand, it is certain that nothing
is more edifying than a Community in which
there is not one individual who would consent
to be an unnecessary exception to the common
order of things in what regards food, clothing,
or aught besides. Undoubtedly, every religious
is strictly obliged not to desire, or even permit
such exceptions; for to do so, would be to
attack religious discipline in its foundations.
What a strange Community, truly, that would
be, where persons might live according to their
fancy, and each follow a different regimen !

The Constitutions mention only exceptions
rendered necessary by ill health, and observe
that it is for the physician and the superiors to
judge of them, not for the other members of the

Community. To murmur at such exceptions,
as the judicious Humbert remarks, is to resemble the selfish, covetous Judas, murmuring on
account of the perfume that Mary Magdalen
poured on the head of Jesus. All ought to
consider that whatever good they do, or desire,
to the sick and infirm, is a service either in deed
or in desire to Jesus. Superiors, especially,
ought to be vigilant in seeing that the sick are
treated with the utmost care and tenderest
affection; that they have an infirmary with
every requisite, in a quiet, retired situation;
that the physician is called in promptly, and,
as has been already said, that all who attend
the sick do so as seeing our Divine Lord in their
person. Superiors ought also to be persuaded,
especially when the illness is of long duration,
that it would be a great error to regard it as
entailing a burden on the Community. It will
be the contrary if the Community manifest
generosity and tenderness towards their invalid
sister; for God in His boundless liberality, will
compensate abundantly for all the expense and
trouble that the illness may cause. The judgments of faith and charity differ widely it is
true from those of the world; but the spirit of

that world, so often condemned by our Saviour, ought not to find entrance into the cloister.

Cantipratus relates a remarkable answer given by a lay-brother, who, being habitually confined to his bed, understood from the not very charitable remarks of his brethren, that he was looked upon as a heavy burden on the house. With perfect calmness, and in a most sweet, recollected manner, the good religious said : " If I only keep our holy Rule as well as I can in the infirmary, and possess my soul in patience, I think I do my Convent more service with God, than if I had money to bestow on it." This pious brother was right, adds the historian ; "for souls have not been created for monasteries, but the monasteries have been founded for souls."

Bear this in mind, you, who are envious and uncharitable ; and dread, lest God punish your jealousy by sending you more serious infirmities than others have to endure. Ah ! far better would it be to entertain sentiments such as those the relatives of Rebecca expressed when they exclaimed : *Thou art our sister—mayest thou increase to thousands ;*[1] that is to say : " My dear sister in Jesus Christ, enjoy your privilege,

[1] Gen. xxiv. 60.

and a thousand times more, which I wish you with all my heart."

" Of what advantage to be chaste, if pride hold dominion over you," says St. Augustine. " As rusts eats into iron," says St. Basil, " so jealousy corrodes the soul. It deprives the lamp of chastity of the oil that feeds it, and prevents that virtue and others from subsisting in their full vigour and integrity ; " so far another Doctor. To all this we may add, that a jealous religious is a trouble to everybody ; that she is her own tormentor, and that as the vice of envy, brother to pride, is proper to the demon, so in mankind, it is a striking sign of reprobation.

" Yes," exclaims St. John Chrysostom, " man acquires a resemblance to God by charity, and, on the contrary, by envy and jealousy he deforms himself to the likeness of the demon."

CHAPTER VII.

OF MODESTY.

" There should be nothing singular in your clothing, and seek not to please by your dress, but by your deportment ; your hair should not appear in any part, and it ought neither be arranged with studied care, nor left in disorder through neglect."

THE Sacred Text tells us that *the attire of the*

body shews what a man is.[1] It follows that the habit of the religious must be a sort of revelation of her interior. The first thing required of the Spouse of Christ in this respect is, that there be nothing in her dress that marks a worldly spirit; but that neatness, humility, and holy poverty appear in all. Christ our Lord, for love of us, did not hesitate to wear the garb of a fool, and did not refuse to let Himself be stripped of His garments ; and shall His spouse seek anything in the religious dress but humility, poverty, and mortification ? Let her not fail, however, to preserve order and neatness, which well beseem virginal modesty, and powerfully contribute to edification. " A decent and suitable dress," says St. Jerome, " is commendable and necessary for virgins consecrated to God."

The religious habit of the Spouse of Christ is a sort of armour of defence against the darts of the enemy; for the infernal spirits are seized with terror at the very sight of the blessed clothing, all the parts of which signify something that is an object of complacency to

[1] Eccl. xix. 27.

heaven, of comfort and encouragement to the
devout wearer, and of dread and defeat to Satan.
Thus, its black colour denotes contempt of the
world ; the long train is an emblem of the
wood of the cross; the white portions of the dress
signify innocence and simplicity ; the black veil
is the mark of consecration to God, in the spirit
of renunciation and death, by entire devotion to
the one great business of salvation ; the cincture
excites the Spouse of Christ to exact vigilance
in the combat she has to wage with the devil,
the world, and the flesh.

It was thus that God commanded Job to gird
himself, that, like an intrepid warrior, he might
not recoil from the adversities and contradic-
tions raised up by the enemy of souls. The
prophet Elias and St. John the Baptist likewise
wore a girdle, and Christ our Lord exhorts us
Himself, by this comparison, to combat for life
eternal.

The different parts of her dress may also
remind the religious, especially when she rises
in the morning, of several circumstances of the
Passion of her Saviour. Putting on her holy
habit, let her think of the moment when Jesus,
for love of us, was stripped of His garments,

cruelly scourged, and covered with wounds from head to foot; her cincture will reveal to her how the divine Victim was bound with cords, roughly thrown to the ground, and inhumanly dragged through the streets of Jerusalem; and her veil may bring to her mind the agonizing crown of thorns.

These thoughts of the Passion and Death of her Lord, occupying the mind of the religious on awaking, and while dressing, would establish her in a very essential disposition for spending the rest of the day with profit, enabling her to endure with joy, or at least in a spirit of patience and penance, all its labours and trials. "For," according to the words of St. Augustine, "there is nothing that so sweetens the pains and difficulties we meet with in the accomplishment of duty, as the remembrance of what Christ our Lord has suffered for us."

There is another recollection connected with the holy habit, that is fraught with important lessons, namely, that of the inestimable grace of our vocation; the habit, if we wear it worthily, being a certain sign of our predestination, and even of our being called to fill some of the highest places in the kingdom of Heaven.

It is no wonder, then, that fervent religious, before putting it on, are accustomed to kiss it, in order to shew their gratitude for the precious grace of their vocation. In this way the religious dress serves as a continual exhortation to fervour, an armour against temptations, and a means of adorning our souls with the most excellent virtues of humility, patience, renunciation, purity of heart, courage, perseverance, and all others necessary to form the true Spouse of Jesus.

Let each one now ask herself whether she has hitherto worn her holy habit in such a spirit that it has been for her a means of salvation, and a defence against the enemies of her soul; or whether the spirit of the world may not have sought to hide in its sacred folds. Oh, how evil would such an abuse be! What an object of derision to the world and to hell should that religious be, who, for the sake of a few rags of stuff, would consent to forfeit the plenitude of blessings so surely to be hers, did she only value and wear her holy habit as she ought? The prophet Jeremias but too justly deplores this misfortune, crying out: "They that were clothed in silk and purple, are now covered with filth." May God avert such misery from the Spouse of Jesus! May she ever be a truly generous heroine, despising the perverse world which she trampled under foot when she entered her sacred Order ; and still more solemnly at the moment of her holy Profession.

II.

" Seek rather to be in the company of your sisters than alone ; and whether you walk or stand, take care that in your whole demeanour, in every gesture and movement, there may not be anything offensive to the eyes of others ; but all that gravity and modesty suited to the holiness of your state ; and govern your eyes in such a manner that you may never fix them on any person."

No one doubts that the true Spouse of Jesus should love solitude, and should desire to be as often as possible alone with her God ; otherwise she could have no spirit of prayer, no recollection, no fervour, no true religious spirit. However, in the daughters of St. Angela, this love of solitude is to be moderated by their vocation to the active life. It is for them a duty not to allow themselves to be led away by an inordinate love of solitude, or a wish to

be apart from others; but, on the contrary, to
seek the society of their sisters, as is prescribed
by the regulations of the house. Every one
should resolve on the fervent observance of this
point of rule; and all ought to understand,
that if solitude has its advantages and privileges, which the mixed life cannot offer, the
latter has graces and securities vainly to be
sought for in solitude.

St. Bernard remarks that the common life
when well regulated, is a better preventative of
evil than one that is wholly solitary. "A
fault that no one sees," he says, "no one
punishes; and where no chastisement is to be
feared, temptation will present itself more
boldly and more dangerously." In community
life, on the contrary, at least in all well ordered
communities, good is accomplished, and, at the
same time, vigilance is exercised; so that those
whom more perfect motives might not restrain,
are deterred from wrong-doing by the prospect
of penances or reprimands from Superiors. So,
should you be one of the foolish virgins, the
society of your sisters will make you correct
yourself and become one of the wise; and if
you are one of the wise, the society of your

sisters will tend to keep you good; for, abandoned to yourself, you might turn aside into some danger. At the same time it is not to be denied that intercourse with our neighbour is attended with its own perils—therefore, a few rules for our guidance in this matter are necessary.

The first is, that our sisterly intercourse should not be limited to a few individuals, which would cause it to degenerate into particular friendships; we have already shown the great mischief these do in a community.

The second, to preserve in all our words and actions holy simplicity, accompanied with religious modesty and civility. We shall speak first of simplicity or sincerity. Our Saviour teaches it in his holy Gospel: *Let your speech be yea, yea; no, no;*[1] that is, simply according to truth. This is a quality which every religious desires to find in her sisters, for we naturally love to deal with sincere and upright hearts; close, artful reserve is always an element of disunion. A religious sisterhood ought, in this point, to imitate the society of the holy angels

---

[1] St. Matt. v. 37.

of God. There is among them neither false-
hood nor cunning, but they live before the face
of God in the perfect unity of His charity,
each communicating to the others his own
happiness, without deception or disguise.

The simplicity and sincerity of Job are praised
in the Holy Scriptures—*that man was simple and
upright, and fearing God and avoiding evil.*[1] His
innocence of heart, his mildness, circumspection
and modesty, made him wish well to all, give
offence to none, and saved himself from many
dangerous snares.

Always to speak the pure truth, and never to
impose on any one, is to act nobly; and this,
according to St. Bernard, combined with a
sweet, religious gravity, is absolutely necessary for all who live together in community,
so that peace, charity, and union may be
preserved and cemented; and that undue
familiarity may be avoided; but this simplicity
and sincerity must never lead the religious into
imprudence. Our Divine Lord says: *Be ye
wise as serpents, and simple as doves.*[2] It is not
the cunning of the serpent that he recommends,

---

[1] Job, i. 1.   [2] St. Matt. x. 15.

but its foresight ; simplicity, as well as every other virtue, must have its limits. It would be to mistake it grossly, and to turn it to the great disadvantage of our neighbour and ourselves, did we imagine it authorised us to say unreflectingly everything that came into our minds, or rose to our lips. Such a proceeding would find its condemnation in the words of the Apostle St. James : *If any man think himself to be religious, not bridling his tongue, this man's religion is vain.*[1] It is of the highest importance in a convent to know how to govern the tongue, and to abstain from all remarks on one's sisters. Thereby we prevent suspicions and reports that should end in disorder. All that the amiable virtue of simplicity demands of religious is, that their hearts be full of affection and respect for their sisters, and that they converse together frankly and amicably on subjects from which no offence to any one, or other bad effect, need be apprehended.

The second regards the religious modesty and decorum to be observed in our relations with our sisters.

---

[1] St. James, i. 26.

This angelic virtue of modesty, in words and deportment, contributes more to mutual edification and the good of souls, than can be expressed. It is related of St. Lucian, priest and martyr, that his admirable modesty had such power over the pagans that many were converted to the faith; and others feared to look at him, lest the mere sight might make them embrace Christianity. So it is too, that the very appearance of a perfectly modest religious excites the fervour of all. St. Bernard diffused around as much edification by his grave and modest exterior, as by the unction of his mellifluous words.

Everyone knows the blessings that the example of the angelical St. Aloysius drew down on those who saw him either in his college, or in the streets, and how seculars frequented the Jesuits' Church solely to admire the recollection with which he prayed, and approached the Holy Communion.

Exterior modesty requires not only that we govern the tongue, but likewise that we guard the eyes : *By the eyes*, says the Holy Spirit, *death has entered the soul as by a window*.[1]

---

[1] Jer. ix. 21.

St. Augustine says: "Pretend not that thy heart is chaste if thine eyes are impure, for the impure eye is the messenger of an unclean heart."

St. Jerome asserts that the curiosity of the eyes is the origin of impurity. Had David guarded his, he would not have fallen so low. Therefore, let the Spouse of Jesus make a compact with her eyes in imitation of holy Job. Let her keep them habitually lowered, without wandering to the right or left, never fixing them on the person to whom she speaks, especially if that person be a secular.

But this religious modesty must extend to every particular. When the Holy Spirit tells us to beg for *a gate of prudence before our lips;* [1] He adds: *Hedge in thy ears with thorns* [2] that they may not hear idle or evil words. And the Apostle of Nations, addressing us all, says: *Let your modesty be known to all.* [3] The good religious, then, will endeavour to conform all her movements to the rules of this perfect religious modesty. She will not move her head from side to side; or assume at one

time a look of unmeaning presumption; at
another, of deep dejection; but always preserve a tranquil countenance, indicative of a
calm, recollected soul.

When disengaged from work, she will hold
her hands tranquilly, and will not swing her
arms when walking. Her gait will be moderate;
her head held neither too high nor too low, but
slightly inclined. Every part of her dress will
be neat, and arranged according to established
custom; much mutual edification is hereby
given in religious life. But on the contrary,
where the helm of this holy modesty is lost, the
vessel of the religious state must suffer ship-
wreck.

Religious are not to touch each other " even
in jest;" meeting through the house, &c., they
are to render mutual marks of esteem and deference, as charity and politeness require. A
community in which the holy rule is observed
will be saintly even as to the exterior, and the
words of our Lord will find in it their verification : *So let your light shine before men .   .   .
that they may glorify your Father who is in Heaven.*[1]

---

[1] St. Matt. v. 16.

The sentence of the Apostle may also be justly applied to it: *We are the good odour of Christ unto God.*[1]

CHAPTER VIII.

OF THE FEAR OF GOD.

Let those who fail in their duty not endeavour to hide their faults, nor rejoice at not having been seen ; for when they least expect it their failings will be discovered. They may indeed conceal what they have done from creatures, but how could they do so from that Eye which beholds all things here below? Shall anyone dare to say that He does not see it, He who looks down upon all things with as much patience as wisdom. Every religious should, therefore, fear to displease Him in order to please creatures ; and should remember that He beholds all things. Thus will she be able to overcome the inordinate dread of being observed by others. For this reason has the fear of God been recommended to us."

Do no evil, and no evil shall lay hold of thee,[2] says the Holy Spirit by the mouth of the Wise Man. The Apostle also exhorts us through the same Holy Spirit : *Giving no offence to any one.*[3] It

---

[1] 2 Cor. ii. 15.   [2] Eccles. vii. 1.   [3] 2 Cor. vi. 3.

would assuredly be best for us if our conduct
were at all times blameless ; and each one ought
earnestly endeavour to attain to this degree.
Nevertheless, however great our care may be,
we all fall, on account of human weakness.
But let no deliberate malice be found in the
failings which occur in convents. Unhappily,
the contrary is often the case. When religious
discipline begins to decay in a monastery, failings occur not merely in a few things; but
the sins of the religious become more numerous
and grave than those even of worldlings.
Why? because their abuse of grace is far
greater. Therefore it is that St. Augustine
says: "I have never found better nor worse
persons than in convents." This is true, for the
higher is the state of the religious (and it is so
high as even to approach the condition of the
angels), so much the deeper, more terrible and
ruinous is her fall.

There are no more powerful means of preventing the possibility of so great an evil, than
for the religious to walk continually in the
presence of God, and mutually to correct each
other's failings, in the spirit of fraternal charity
for others usually perceive our faults more

clearly than we can see them ourselves. We have proof of how powerful a means of preserving the soul from falling into sin in the time of temptation is the remembrance of the Presence of God, from the examples of Joseph in Egypt, and of the chaste Susanna. Both were strongly tempted, and both were victorious, because they were mindful of it in the moment of trial. *How then can I do this wicked thing, and sin against my God,*[1] exclaimed Joseph, and thus he conquered. *But it is better for me to fall into your hands without doing it, than to sin in the sight of the Lord,*[2] cries out Susanna, and she too won the victory. It is much easier for a religious to resist temptation by the thought of the Divine Presence, than it was for Joseph and Susanna—for she has not, as they had, to fear exterior violence. Rightly does St. John Chrysostom say: "As soldiers and guards drive away robbers, so does the remembrance of God's holy presence drive away all sin." The just in the Old Law were diligent in this exercise, as we learn from the prayer of the patriarch Jacob: *O God, in whose sight my fathers*

---

[1] Gen. xxxix. 9.   [2] Dan. xiii. 23.

Abraham and Isaac walked.[1] This practice is a
no less powerful incentive to the acquisition of
every virtue. For when does a soldier fight
more bravely, when does a servant work more
diligently than when his leader or master looks
on? And when does a child obey more perfectly than when his actions are done in
sight of his father? God himself gave this
means of acquiring sanctity to the patriarch and
father of true believers, Abraham, in the words:
Walk before me and be perfect.[2] As if he had
said: "You will be perfect if you remember
my presence at all times." For the same reason
old Tobias gave his son the following important
lesson: *And all the days of thy life keep God in
thy mind, and desire of Him to direct all thy
ways, and that all thy counsels may abide in
Him.*[3] David also says: *Set the Lord always
in my sight, for He is at my right hand, that I be
not moved: therefore my heart hath been glad,
and my tongue hath rejoiced.*[4] These happy
effects will also be experienced by the religious
who is mindful of the divine Presence.

---

[1] Gen. xlviii. 15.   [2] Gen. xvii. 1.   [3] Tob. iv. 6. 20.
[4] Ps. xv. 8, 9.

" Truly," says St. Dorotheus, " nothing so strengthens and refreshes the soul as the constant remembrance of the presence of God ; by it she is urged to prove herself courageous in combating against her passions; for with it is joined that holy fear of which it is written : *No evil shall happen to him that feareth the Lord ; but in temptation God will keep him, and deliver him from evil.*"[1] As to the practice, there is no real difficulty in acquiring it ; for it is not necessary to make any violent efforts to direct the intention, but simply from time to time to make an act of faith, even in thought. Whoever accustoms herself to say often with mind and heart : " God sees me," will soon become recollected, and will walk continually in the presence of her Lord and God.

We have already spoken on the happiness which the practice of this virtue ought to cause to the Spouse of Christ, because it is an indispensable condition for contemplation and communication with God in the interior life. We now speak of it only as the strongest means of

[1] Eccles. xxxiii. 1.

resisting temptation, and preserving the soul from falling into sin; which grace may God grant unto us all.   Amen.

CHAPTER IX.

OF FRATERNAL CORRECTION.

" If you remark in one of your sisters a notable fault, warn her of it immediately, in order that of her own accord she may correct herself without delay, and that thus the beginning may not be permitted to increase. But if immediately after being warned, or some days after, you perceive that she relapses, whoever sees the act will denounce it and discover it, as that of a sick person, in order that a cure may be provided. It would be well to expose the matter to one or two, that the sister may, if necessary, be convicted by the testimony of two or three, and then punished with proportionate severity."

A CHARITABLE word of correction, received with gratitude and humility, is the most powerful means of raising a person from any fault or sin, and of preventing relapses. It is the unanimous opinion of the Fathers of the Church that we are all obliged to contribute it, especially in the case of any serious fault.   And to support their doctrine they appeal, with St. Thomas of Aquin, to these words of our Lord related by St. Matthew: *If thy brother shall offend against thee, go and rebuke him between thee and him alone. If he shall hear thee, thou shalt gain thy brother. And if he will not hear thee, take with thee one or two more, that in the mouth of two or three witnesses every word may stand. And if he will not hear them, tell the Church. And if he will not hear the Church, let him be to thee as the heathen and publican.*[1]

These words of the Saviour clearly point out the duty of fraternal correction, and the order to be observed in making it; since by the commandment of the love of our neighbour, we are obliged to interest ourselves for his salvation as for our own. This duty becomes more strict in proportion as our neighbour's connection with us is closer. It is consequently very obligatory on religious who are to spend their lives in the cloister, under the same holy roof. Even one serious fault might become for a community, a scandal, the consequences of which would be incalculable.

[1] St. Matt. xviii. 15, 16, 17.

But, in order that mutual correction may be profitable and attain its end, there are some rules to be observed ; of those the following are the principal :—

1. The correction should at first be in private, at a seasonable time, and after having prepared the offender for it. You violate this rule by imprudent, unreflecting, and public censure, given at the moment a fault is committed. And should the person whom you reprimand not have failed in presence of those who hear the correction, you have to answer for the injury done to her character, and it may be in a matter of importance.

2. Before reprehending any one, see that you are in a proper disposition for doing so, to good purpose. Prepare your soul; place yourself in the presence of God ; form your intention, and guard against every feeling of bitterness or anger. You should also prepare the person to whom you have to speak, that she may be willing to receive the correction, and be grateful for it.

3. The moment a fault is acknowledged, and readiness expressed to make atonement, the reprimand should end; for St. Ambrose says: "God changes the sentence He had pronounced, as soon as the sinner turns away from his sin."

4. Correction should emanate from a motive of pure charity alone; it should never be given at the dictation of a mind or heart resentful for some injury. She, who, through wounded pride or self-love, blames the conduct of her neighbour, instead of exciting sorrow for the fault, whatever it may be, and a desire of repairing it, will rather arouse a spirit of obstinacy and untractableness. Thus, trouble and unkind feeling spring up, where only the effects of tender charity should be seen.

Our holy Father, St. Augustine, says: "Why do you exhort your brother? Is it not perhaps because he has pained or offended you? If so, it is mere nature that inspires you, and you can do no good; but if, on the contrary, you speak through a sentiment of charity, your reprehension will avail much."

5. Before censuring others, examine closely
whether you have not the same defect
that you seek to correct in them. For
in such a case it may be said to you:
Physician, heal thyself;[1] and: *Cast first
the beam out of thy own eye.*[2] Here your
correction will have no other effect than
that of embittering minds; unless indeed, you first accuse yourself of the
fault in question; for then you may
venture to admonish others. "How,"
says St. Gregory, "can any one with dust
in his eyes, and mud in his hands, undertake to help his brother, or guide him
in the right way?"

The duty of correction weighs chiefly on the
Superior. Her charge obliges her to keep a
strict watch over the spiritual interests of her
daughters; as having *to render an account*[3] to
God of the souls of all in general, and of each
in particular. It is proper then to let her know
their faults; this should be done especially in
the case of one who will not heed a remonstrance
from other quarters. Usually indeed, this work

---

[1] St. Luke, iv. 23.   [2] St. Luke, vi. 42.   [3] Heb. xiii. 17.

of charity is performed with most facility and
success by the Superior herself. She, consequently, should give her attention, not only
to public faults, but likewise to well-founded
suspicions, taking measures to discover the true
state of things, that she may not merit the reproach of the Lord : *The weak you have not
strengthened, and that which was sick you have not
healed ; that which was broken you have not bound
up, and that which was driven away you have not
brought again ; neither have you sought that which
was lost.*[1] Superiors who fear to offend those
under them by a deserved rebuke, and so leave
their faults unpunished, can apply to themselves
the comparison that the Lord makes by the
mouth of the prophet Isaias : *dumb dogs not able
to bark.*[2] True, such negligent Superiors may
allege specious pretexts for their conduct.
" What is the use," they say, " of so many ad-
monitions ? They end in aversions, ill-will,
complaints and murmurs ; instead of being of
any benefit to the sisters, they only make them
dissatisfied with her," &c. Let those who speak
in such terms reflect on the rejoinder of St.

---

[1] Ezech. xxxiv. 4.   [2] Isaias. lvi. 10.

Gregory: "You seek, it appears," he says, "your own glory, not the glory of God, or the salvation of souls." Far from closing her eyes to faults through any unworthy condescension, a Superior should make those under her charge feel, by her wise and charitable counsel or reproof, that she has their spiritual good at heart. And if in exercising this point of fraternal love, as required by holy Rule, the recommendations here given be observed, peace, concord, and edification will result, not murmuring or discontent.

To what has been already said on the subject it is unnecessary to add, that private correction and reprehension will not always suffice. When a fault is public, or of a nature to injure or disedify a community, the satisfaction for it should be made in public, always taking care that the delinquent be well disposed for it. This manner of repairing offences against the Rule, or others more serious, when conducted with prudence and vigour, has often had the most excellent effect on those who gave occasion for it, and on many besides—according to the words of the Apostle: *Them that sin reprove before all : that the rest also may have fear.*[1] In this, as in all

---

[1] 1 Tim. v. 20.

else, discretion and charity are to be observed ; whilst, on the other hand, there is to be no conniving at any violation of religious discipline, which, if left unredressed, would soon bring on its complete decay. Finally, under all critical and difficult circumstances, let us ever remember that even from evil God can draw good. Amen.

II.

" And do not suppose that you show a want of affection to her whom you accuse, for if, in being silent you allow your sister to perish, whom you might have corrected by discovery, you become guilty of that fault. If any person had a wound in her body which she wished to hide through fear of an incision, would it not be cruel of you to conceal it, and charitable to discover it? How much more necessary for you to make known her spiritual wound, lest a more dangerous corruption may be engendered in her soul? In case that she denies the fact, before confronting her with the others who are to convict her, let her be brought before the Mother Superior, that being reprehended privately, fewer persons may know the fault. If she deny it then, let the others be brought in, that she may not alone be accused by one witness, but convicted in the presence of all, on the testimony of two or three."

Blessed are they that suffer persecution for justice sake,[1] says our Lord Jesus Christ. A

[1] St. Matt v. 10.

fervent religious ought to bear a singular affection to this promise of the Saviour, in order that she may not trouble herself, or grieve too much about it, should she have anything of the kind to suffer from an imperfect or degenerate sister. For the discharge of the duty of fraternal correction may expose her to vexations; nay, even to persecution. However, she is not to be uneasy though she should be regarded as one, who, by discovering the shortcomings of her sisters, sought to gain favour with her Superior; or of whom even a more injurious opinion might be held. If good Christians in the world have to suffer patiently for justice sake, much more are religious bound to it, having so many efficacious helps for turning it to the profit of their own souls, and the souls of others. Yes, it happens not unfrequently, that those who were the most averse to reproof, enter into themselves, and understanding the real charity that has been done them, become sincerely attached to those who rescued them from danger; whilst they lose all confidence in the Superior and sisters who had negligently overlooked their faults.

We shall remark here that in the accusation

of faults, there are some rules which it is essential to observe :—

1. The matter should be of such importance as to deserve the notice of the Superior. Representations made about trifles are no proof of pure charity, but rather of minds possessed by envy, jealousy, or an idle love of talk, and the fruits must necessarily be bad.

2. The same method and order are to be followed, and the same motives are to influence us, that have been detailed in the paragraphs on correction of faults; in this way the salutary end we have in view will be attained.

3. It is right to know that Superiors themselves are amenable to this law, if guilty of grievous transgressions which might scandalize, or be greatly prejudicial to a community.

It is in the interests of Superiors that this duty of charity should be exercised when rendered necessary. How unfortunate for them if their elevated changes deprived them of this great spiritual good. In that case their subjects would be far better off than they.

It is, no doubt, superfluous to add, that all remonstrances made to Superiors, should be accompanied with profound respect, and preceded by fervent prayer. And as it is natural to shrink from pointing out to those over us, the faults we may observe in them, it behooves a Superior, who is zealous for her perfection, to let her sisters understand that she is ready to hear what they disapprove of in her conduct, and willing to rectify it if needful. Yet more, I should say that a Superior ought to appoint some sister to observe, and inform her if she or others have any cause of complaint against her.

This has been done even by holy Bishops, as for instance, St. Charles Borromeo, who charged two of his priests to keep a continual watch over him. In some Orders, too, it forms a particular point in the Rules and Constitutions. And certainly if a Superior reflect often on the grave sentence of the Holy Scripture: *A most severe judgment shall be for them that bear rule,*[1] she will be all zeal and solicitude to procure for herself the great benefit of fraternal correction, and through it, to draw upon herself numberless heavenly favours; for it is written: *God gives His grace to the humble.*[2] Amen.

[1] Wis. vi. 6.   [2] St. James, iv. 6 & 1 Ep. Pet. v. 5.

III.

"Being convicted, the judgment and discretion of the Mother, or Father Superior, will decide the penance or chastisement she is to suffer for the fault. If she refuse to receive this penance, she should, not through cruelty, but through charity, be separated from the others that she may not destroy many by her pestilential contagion."

All that we have hitherto said of fraternal correction, proves the importance of this duty in the religious state, especially in what concerns Superiors. They should, therefore, make themselves acquainted with the faults of those under their care. As St. Gregory says: "It is no excuse for a shepherd that it was without his knowledge that a wolf devoured the sheep." But on the other hand, inferiors are not less bound to accept and be grateful for the solicitude and corrections of the Superior, even though it might appear to them that these exceeded what was justly their due. For, if the religious who is thus unfairly penanced, be worthy of her name, and a true imitator of Jesus, she will rejoice exceedingly to be in some respect conformable to the Lamb without spot, the innocent by

excellence, submitting to an iniquitous condemnation, and by His divine humility con-
quering pride. Let her, then, keep her eyes
fixed on her crucified Saviour, to whom she is
united by the sacred bonds of a chaste alliance,
and whom she must resemble, in order that He
may abide in her for ever. Moreover, by the
patient endurance of an undeserved reprimand,
she gains a great and real advantage, which is
that of being more on her guard than she had
previously been, against the fault of which she
has been wrongfully accused. Who can say
that God has not permitted the correction as a
preservative, so that she, now blameless, might
not commit a fault of that very kind at a later
time.

Then we should remember that it is very
pleasing to God, and very meritorious, that we
should bear to be unjustly punished ; in His
most pure and holy eyes, it surpasses the value
of fasts and disciplines.

A soul may be assured of diminishing thereby the pains that await her in Purgatory ; perhaps even of obtaining their total remission.

St. Peter Damian says, and experience confirms it, that she likewise breaks all the power

and violence of temptation. Let her think besides on the doctrine of our holy Father St. Augustine. He tells us that a religious Order is maintained principally by the observance of the three following points : A pious zeal for the adornment of the church, and for the divine service ; lively and charitable solicitude for the poor ; and exact care to impose penance for faults, especially for violations of holy Rule.

It seems to us that any religious, who maturely weighs the foregoing considerations, must be prepared to resolve generously, despite the repugnances of nature, to accept patiently, and even joyfully, every correction, whether merited or not. She will also resolve never to excuse herself, unless there be an evident necessity, and that it can be done so as to leave her calm of soul undisturbed. She should speak only after having listened to her Superior in profound and respectful silence ; then, if she have any explanation to offer, let her give it, according as truth and the good edification of the community require. Should she have to do herself great violence, let her remember these words of the great Apostle : *Watch ye, stand fast in the faith, do manfully, and be strengthened. Let all your works be done in charity.*[1]   Amen.

IV.

"And this mode of action should be carefully followed out in the seeking out, conviction, and correction of all faults; but let it ever be with great love of the persons, and hatred only of their vices."

Our Holy Father here supplies Superiors with a rule for their guidance. If faithfully adhered to, it will teach them the exact measure of the correction to be used, and how to administer it. It must be with love for the persons, and hatred of their vices.

To comply with the first condition, they need only ask themselves how they would penance a dearly loved relative, and they will immediately discover the just measure, both as to the degree of chastisement, and the manner of imposing it.

The Hermits of St. Augustine have a very wise and commendable Constitution, which

---

[1] 1 Cor. xvi. 13, 14.

obliges the Superior, before enjoining any hard penance, to confer on the subject with some other Father, who is distinguished for prudence, zeal, and piety. He has to ask his advice in this important matter, in order that he may not act precipitately, or allow himself to be carried away by excessive zeal, and, perhaps, cause the person condemned to appeal to the higher Superiors of his Order, a course which commonly leads to disputes, aversions, and dangerous divisions. Whereas, if all be done in the manner here indicated, inferiors will readily submit to the penance imposed, seeing that it is just, and such as the nature of their fault requires.

However, were a religious so forgetful of the sacred duties of her vocation, as to refuse submission, some salutary severity should be employed with holy firmness. The Rule orders her to be separated from the others. This, however, is a measure that ought not to be resorted to, without first informing the Father Superior, in order to be more certain of attaining the desired end, which is, with holy authority, to reduce the erring, and preserve others from the contagion of bad example, by a wholesome fear of similar falls.

As to the subjects for accusation and correction, they comprehend not only violations of the laws of God and of His Church; but likewise, all faults against Holy Rule and religious discipline.

CHAPTER X.

OF LETTERS AND PRESENTS.

"If any one go so far as to commit the grievous fault of receiving a letter or present privately, and that of her own accord she confesses it, pardon her, and pray to God for her. But if she should be surprised in the fact, she ought to be punished more severely, according to the prudence of the Mother Superior, or as the Father Superior, or even the Bishop may judge necessary."

ACCORDING to the Rule of St. Augustine there is question here of presents given, or received in private, as well as of letters written secretly.

With regard to presents, all know that it is unlawful for any religious, without the express leave of her Superior, to give or receive presents; that being contrary to the vow of Holy Poverty.

Nor should a religious think it in the slightest degree a hardship, that a present made to her should be given to another, or distributed among the whole community by the Superior. To repine at this would be to fail, not only against poverty, but also against obedience and fraternal charity.

Concerning letters, it is to be observed, and it can be easily understood, that a free correspondence would expose a religious soul to many dangers, and open in the monastery a wide door for worldly vanities. Hence the necessity for the wise regulation that religious should not write letters without permission from the Superior to whom they will give them to be sealed with the convent seal. All letters addressed to them are also to pass through the Superior, who will open them and give them or not, according as she judges proper. In this, as well as in all that concerns correction, moderation and wise circumspection are to be exercised, according to the diversity of characters and circumstances. This is confirmed by the words of our Holy Father St. Augustine. He says, it is well to note how far a person has failed, and what gave occasion to the fault; how this fault itself may be most easily corrected; what the dispositions of the culprit are, and whether she is more to be excused or blamed.

Then all must be poised in a just balance; reason being the weight to be used—and finally what seems the best course to be decided on.

Concluding this chapter we shall remind the Spouse of Jesus, of the important virtue of humility, which is so necessary to enable one to take corrections patiently. Let her make frequent and deep reflections on this truth, that she can hardly work out her salvation in the religious state unless she endeavour to become humble of heart, and to look on herself as the last of all. Let her be strongly persuaded that she has not entered religion to command, but to obey; not to be exalted, but on the contrary to be abased; not to be served, but to serve; not to be at her ease, but to do penance; not to flatter nature and follow its dictates, but to die to self and to live hidden with Christ in God; not to give free scope to her tongue, but to observe silence; not to rejoice, but to suffer, and through many trials and tribulations to enter into everlasting felicity. Finally, let her remember that her life and her works will be agreeable to God, and meritorious in His eyes, only in proportion as she shall humble herself profoundly before Him and before all her sisters.

CHAPTER XI.

OF CLOTHING AND NEATNESS.

"Let all your clothes be kept in one place, and under the care of one or two, or of as many as may be required to clean and keep them from moths. And as you receive all necessary food from one cellar, so, your clothing should be got from one wardrobe. Give yourself no anxiety about being clothed according to the season, or of getting again the same articles which you had left off before, instead of what others had worn ; but be satisfied if you want nothing necessary."

THE term clothing includes here, all that according to the Rules and Constitutions of the Order is to serve for the covering of the body. We have already spoken of the parts that compose it, and have said that it is to be an exterior sign of humility and renunciation of worldly pomps and vanities, to which renunciation we are specially obliged by the religious state.

This clothing is to be furnished to the religious by the convent itself. It would be a culpable and most dangerous deviation from

rule to give individuals an annual sum of money
with which to procure habits, &c. This would
be to give rise to a sort of proprietary; and instead of the spirit of Jesus Christ, the miserable
spirit of Judas would insinuate itself into the
Community, with deplorable consequences, from
which may Almighty God ever preserve us all.

It is rarely allowed to religious to have even
the care of their own habits. All, according to
the express command of the holy rule, should be
kept in one wardrobe, and distributed as occasion
may require. The case would be different were
the convent unable to afford the sisters the
necessary supply of clothing ; each should then
get permission to procure it for herself, a case
unusual in these countries. But even under such
circumstances, she should still consider her clothing not as her own, but as the property of the
monastery; and the same is to be said of everything else that she has for her use.

Bearing on this matter, there exists a very
excellent custom in some Orders, as, for instance,
that of the Visitation. Every year the religious
exchange with one another all that they have
for their use, a few trifles excepted ; so as to
preserve no attachment to anything whatsoever,

whether cell, picture, or beads, &c.—for even such objects may prove obstacles to the attainment of perfection. In other Orders the religious usually collect their books, with whatever else may compose their pious store, and lay all together on the Superior's table. It is for her then to distribute them anew; which she does indiscriminately, without even looking at what comes under her hand.

God grant that, at least, the spirit of holy detachment from the smallest things, may be found in every religious house; so that each of the Spouses of Jesus may be able to exclaim with truth, and from her inmost soul: "My God *is* my all!" Amen.

———

II.

"If murmurs or disputes arise on this matter, so that any-one complains of getting worse than she had before, and if she says that she does not deserve to be more poorly clad than another, by all that you may well perceive how much you want the interior sanctity of the soul's clothing, since you take such trouble about the covering of your body."

Too great an attachment to terrestrial things,

says St. Augustine, is a source of spiritual torment and discontent. Good religious are always in the disposition that St. Paul requires in every true Christian, when he says : *Having food and raiment we are content.*[1] In a very particular manner this satisfied spirit ought to be discernible amongst religious, who, in consequence of their vow of poverty, have no right to look on anything as their own.

If, then, a religious has no right to anything, how can she complain when she is not served as she would wish ? Truly, there can be nothing more scandalous than to hear of such complaints in a convent. The malice of the vice becomes more apparent from the fact, that this murmuring is generally indulged in places where it ought not be breathed, and in presence of persons who have not the requisite knowledge or ability to remedy matters; whence ensues a more embittered state of feeling than existed before.

Even though a religious should render external submission to an unpleasant order, if she murmur while executing it, she becomes a

---

[1] Tim. vi. 8.

disturber of the peace of her monastery, and burdens herself with a great responsibility before God. And even were the murmuring altogether interior, the injury she does her soul is still very considerable, for her peace of mind is destroyed; and in that state there can be for her no union with God, or participation in the true religious life, so rich in virtues, graces, and heavenly benedictions.

St. Augustine enters into a transport of holy anger against this pest of the monastic profession, and warns us to defend ourselves from the spirit of murmuring and discontent, under penalty of God's severest judgments. He plainly declares that a religious under its influence cannot please God, what efforts soever she may make. "For," adds St. Basil, "the murmurer is not obedient, and the Lord consequently rejects her service and her sacrifices." He Himself testified His abhorrence of this vice by the awful miracle of the sudden leprosy, with which He struck Mary, the sister of Moses, for murmuring against the holy Legislator.

It is incredible with what rapidity the leprosy of discontent gains ground, attacking different members of a community like a cancer We meet with some very grave and severe words in St. Augustine's writings on the subject: "An adulteress," he says, "terrified at the shame of crime, is more easily converted, than a religious who has accustomed herself to the impiety of murmuring." Spouse of Jesus, if rash enough to murmur, behold what you are in the eyes of this great doctor!

But if, indeed, a religious happen to be really overburdened, let her represent it in all simplicity, and with submission to her Superiors; and then accommodate herself humbly to their decision and will. Amen.

III.

"When it happens that your own habits are left for you, those which you leave off should be kept in the same place with the others, and by the same persons, so that no one may work, or do any matter in particular for herself either as to dress, bedding, cincture, or veils; but let al your work be done in common, with more care and joy than if it were done for self. Of charity it is written that *it seeketh not its own;* it discovers and manifests itself by preferring that which is in common, to that which is its own; and not that which is its own to what is in common.

" In proportion as you take care of all that is in common, rather than of what is for individual use, you will perceive the progress that you shall have made ; and in consequence it will be evident, that charity, which is permanent, will ever hold the first rank, and that it will appear even in the use of those things that relieve our passing necessities.

" Whatever seculars give to their daughters, relatives, or other religious, whether these presents be clothing or other necessaries of life, they must not be received for private use, but left in the hands of the Mother Superior, that being put in common, they may be used when wanted. If anyone conceals what has been given her, she should be condemned as guilty of theft."

Self-interest, which is another name for self-love, is the root of all evil, as charity is the source and principle of all good. How strong and true this charity is, will be proved in the religious state, principally by a love for the common life, which is to be evinced by zeal in promoting the welfare of the community, and labouring diligently to this effect. It is a good sign when a religious devotes herself willingly to some toilsome and continuous occupation for the benefit of her convent ; but a bad sign, on the contrary, if she is prompt and painstaking to provide for her own necessities, and indolent and careless about what concerns the community.   We ought to employ every precaution against this evil. " It is such a common thing," St. Leo says, " to labour through inclination and self-interest, rather than for love of virtue."

The rule adds, that a religious cannot consider as her own, anything that may be given to her by seculars ; that all those presents belong to the community, and are to be dispensed by order of the Superior.

Since all is to be in common, it follows, that no one should bring anything with her from the world to be used as her own property. This is not permitted by the vow of poverty, any more than by divine charity, which is the soul of the religious state.

The first Christians had *but one heart and one soul*, as the Acts of the Apostles bear testimony, and it was this spirit of charity that introduced among them a community of goods. So long as they persevered in that holy custom, charity suffered no diminution; but in their case, no less than with the world at large, the use of the cold words *mine* and *thine*, as St. John Chrysostom energetically declares, opened the way for discord. Founders of religious orders have preserved a practice, which, owing to the want of perfect charity, can no longer exist among the generality of the faithful, and have made it a strict obligation for souls that aspire to perfection in the monastic state.

St. Augustine insists, in a special manner, on the observance of this rule : "You are not to possess anything as your own." It is a subject of extreme amazement, that there should be religious who would scruple omitting some little prayer they had promised to God, and yet would expose themselves, without much concern, to the danger of violating their vow of holy poverty.

Such inconsistent persons ought to reflect on the terrible punishment with which God visited Ananias and Saphira, when, in the community of the first Christians, they sought to retain something as their own. He, by St. Peter's ministry, suddenly struck them dead ; and yet they were not so strictly obliged as religious are, to the common life. We know with what severity the Fathers of the Desert punished violations of the vow of poverty. As has been already said, if it was discovered, after a monk's death, that he had been a proprietor, instead of burying him in consecrated ground, they threw his corpse, with the money found in his possession, into some filthy hole, as things accursed. Our Lord Himself says : *Unless you renounce all that you possess, you cannot be my disciples.*[1]

Religious who act contrary to this maxim expose their salvation to great danger. However irreproachable their exterior conduct may be, if they fail against holy poverty and charity, in so essential a point, we must apply to them the words of the Apostle : *Though I should speak with the tongues of angels, if I have not charity I am become as sounding brass, or a tinkling cymbal.*[2] With all their show of renunciation and religious discipline, they are in the sight of God mere hollow vessels, void of any merit. The desire of possessing robs them of all their spiritual gains. It is truly surprising how the enemy can thus lead religious, who abandoned much of the world's wealth, to set a value, in the convent, on perhaps some worthless little piece of serge ; and for sake of that, to expose themselves to greater danger of losing their souls, than while they were in the midst of riches. Those, on the contrary, who

[1] St. Luke, xiv. 33.   [2] 1 Cor. xiii. 2.

love the common life, and faithfully follow it, will be found no less good and fervent in every other respect; they follow the exhortation of the Apostle, when he says : *Let us consider one another to provoke unto charity and to good works : not forsaking our assembly.*[1] It is for each, then, to examine herself on this important point, and to remember what has been said elsewhere, that victories over nature in this matter are very pleasing to God, and prepare us to receive the peace of Christ, without which there can be no happiness in this life, but which is impossible to a heart that covets any earthly possession. St. Augustine remarks : "It is less difficult to do without a thing, than to deny ourselves a desire for it." And St. Bernard says justly : "There is nothing so miserable as to seek, and to be attached to what ends with time ; and nothing more consoling than neither to have, nor desire to have, any earthly possession."

---

[1] Heb. x. 24, 25.

IV.

"The habits that you leave off at different seasons should be cleaned and mended, either by yourselves or by others, as the Mother Superior directs, lest too great a desire of neatness in your clothing may create interior filt in your soul."

We have already spoken of the necessity of neatness in the religious dress, and have strongly recommended it. The concluding words of this article of the Holy Rule give occasion to our adding something with regard to the measure to be observed in this particular, and the excesses to be avoided.

Great care should be had of neatness, from a love for purity; never from a desire of pleasing creatures. May God preserve us from such, as it is one of the inclinations most opposed to purity of heart. Such attention to neatness in person and dress, leading to the superfluous use of clean linen, &c., might engender real and great impurity of soul. Let every religious keep constantly in mind these words of the Apostle: *Do I seek to please men? If I yet pleased men, I should not be the servant of Christ.*[1]

[1] Gal. i. 10.

How much more impressively may she say: "If I pleased men, or sought to please them, I should not be a true Spouse of Jesus Christ;" for the virgin sees and hears what is of God, what is of Christ, not what savours of the vanities of the world.

Besides, is she not clothed in that heavenly nuptial robe which has been washed in the Blood of the Lamb, in the Precious Blood that Jesus, her Spouse, shed in the cruel torments of His Passion, and when dying on the Cross? Ah! how could she contemplate her Saviour covered from head to foot with frightful wounds, clothed in a vile purple robe, and presented to the people with the contemptuous words: BEHOLD THE MAN; or see Jesus hanging naked on the wood of the Cross, and think herself like Him, and worthy of her vocation, while she is studying how to set off her person? Indeed, she should have completely forgotten that by her divine alliance with Jesus Crucified, she has contracted the sacred and permanent obligation of living solely for His good pleasure, and not for the favourable opinion of the world.

Let each, then, moved by a spirit of religious

11

modesty, purity of heart, and obedience, endeavour to observe the rules of neatness in all,
especially in her dress, rejecting every kind of
worldly vanity as a folly which even seculars
would think her to be despised and pitied for
indulging; but how much worse would it
appear in the eyes of the celestial court. Let
her not forget the words of Holy Scripture:
But what went you out to see? A man clothed in
soft garments? Behold, they that are clothed in
soft garments are in the houses of kings.[1] And
not in my house.

We shall mention here a great fault against
charity, which arises from over particularity,
perhaps also from vanity. Some religious add
very unnecessarily to the labours of their sisters
in the laundry and other departments, not so
much in the interests of cleanliness, as through
carelessness or to gratify a fancy. They should
know that to act thus is directly contrary to
charity; for it easily brings on disputes and
disagreements, when things are found not to
suit all parties.

Even in this point the prudence and discretion of your glorious father, St. Augustine

---

[1] St. Matt. xi. 8.

furnish you with a model. His attire was exceedingly neat, but quite simple. You may also form an idea of what your Holy Mother St. Angela's deportment would be, and how she would act if in your place; and then imagine she says, in the words of the Apostle: *Be ye imitators of me.*' Amen.

CHAPTER XII.

OF THE CARE OF THE SICK, AND THE WANTS OF THE SISTERHOOD.

" If any sick person require assistance, it ought not to be deferred, but given without murmur, according to the advice of the physician; even though she should not wish it, the Mother Superior ought to insist upon her doing what is necessary for her health. But if she should desire what is not necessary, she should not be gratified; because we are inclined to regard as salutary that which pleases us, though it should be hurtful.

" If the servant of God have any hidden bodily infirmity, she should be believed, nor should it be doubted that she suffers; but in order to be certain whether the relief which she desires be calculated to promote a cure, the physician ought to be consulted when there is no other certainty."

ACCORDING to the doctrine and example of St.

1 Cor. iv. 10.

Paul, the principal exercise of charity consists in feeling for our neighbour's pains and afflictions, as if we were suffering them ourselves. *Who is weak, and I am not weak?*[1] But we must go still farther; it is our Divine Lord Himself whom we are to consider and to care in the person of the sick and afflicted. From his adorable lips the consoling words have come : *I was sick and you visited me. . . . Amen, I say to you, as long as you did it to one of these, my least brethren, you did it to me.*[2]

As to the sick in convents, they may be divided into three classes.

The first is composed of these mortified religious, who, disregarding their infirmities, never think about seeking for remedies or alleviation.

The Superior is bound to be solicitous for such persons, and to use her authority in requiring them to grant to their bodies necessary relief and ease. The good religious, on her side, submits with alacrity, in a spirit of humility and obedience, to every regulation of her Superior. To hold to her own views, contrary to an order intimated, how gently soever, and

---

[1] 2 Cor. xi. 29.   [2] St. Matt. xxv. 36-40.

to persist in mortifying herself, would be the opposite of an act of virtue; it would be very dangerous obstinacy, and most displeasing to God.

We read in the life of St. Nicholas Tolentine, that during a severe illness, the physician, who almost despaired of his recovery, wished him to eat meat. It was contrary to the custom of his Order, and the saint declared he preferred to die keeping his holy rule. However, the Superior having desired him to follow the doctor's prescription, he at once obeyed, and had no sooner tasted the meat than he was cured. Almighty God thus rewarded his humble obedience.

We read, it is true, of saints such as St. Euphrasia, and the great St. Anthony, who had renounced the use of all rare and costly remedies, and abstained from them through a spirit of mortification. We may admire them for it, but they are not in this point models for our imitation. Our perfection consists in submitting humbly to the will of our Superiors, and we shall honour God more by the renunciations we practice by our submission, than we could by the greatest austerities.

The second class of invalids presents a total contrast to the first. It is made up of the cowardly and the fastidious. At every little indisposition they give the alarm, and think it too bad unless the doctor is sent for at once. Then they easily dispense themselves from the observances, on the plea of such very weak health! Moreover, all that composes the ordinary fare of the house disagrees completely with them. Such souls are thus rallied by St. Bernard : " What ! " he says, " is it possible there is nothing to be found good enough for you in the gardens,or in the cellar ? Pray, remember, that you are a monk, not a professor of medicine; and that people come to monasteries less to live according to the constitution they have derived from nature, than according to their religious profession ; therefore, have some compassion on your conscience. You might also, instead of being exclusively taken up with self, cast your eyes on those who sit at table with you, and who are so well satisfied with whatever is presented to them."

From whence are wars and contentions among you ? writes the Apostle St. James. *Come they not hence. From your concupiscences which war in your members.*[1]

---

[1] St. James iv. 1.

With regard to those who erroneously imagine themselves so delicate, the Superior should endeavour to undeceive them, as far as characters and circumstances permit, and especially by means of the physician's authority, so that they may not become an unreasonable burden on her and the community.

The third class of sick religious consists of those who always follow the excellent middle way, and who, without taking notice of any trivial ailments, make known their state when really ill, and frankly ask for what they really require. It is evident that a Superior is bound in conscience, to believe them, and to assist them with very great charity and the utmost care.

Yes, if merely to visit the sick, is in itself a good work, so pleasing to God that the Kingdom of Heaven is promised as its reward; and if our Blessed Lord assures us that it is He, Himself, whom we care and tend in the person of the poor and of the least of his followers, there can be no doubt whatever of the verification of these blessed words when the sick are his own spouses, called by divine and most signal graces to serve Him faithfully in the holy state of religion.

II.

"One of the Sisters ought to be appointed to have care of the sick, and of those who begin to recover health after sickness, in order that she may get from the Depository whatever may be necessary for each one."

What has been already said of the charitable care to be bestowed on the sick, makes known both the merit and the sacred obligations of the Infirmarian's office. Assuredly, she to whom this sweet and important charge is confided, should rejoice very much at being able to testify her love for Jesus in so efficacious and consoling a manner.

One day a venerable religious was addressed by a young brother as follows: "Father, there are in our Order two monks, one of whom fasts rigidly, and labours incessantly; the other serves the sick and infirm with unwearying zeal. Which of the two will have the greater reward?" The saint answered without a moment's hesitation, that the latter was the more rich in merit, because of his zeal in exercising what was peculiarly a work of charity; charity being the compendium and fulfilment of the law.

In truth, since the Divine Saviour promised

heaven to the charitable souls who visit the
sick, the measure of His rewards must be boundless for those who devote themselves to their
service, embracing all the sacrifices and all
the abnegation which that service commonly
entails.

The enlightened Doctor, St. Bonaventure,
penetrated with the force of such reasons as we
have been stating, applied himself with the
most tender charity to solace his ailing brethren
as far as other employments would permit.   An
infirmarian, who was a very pious man, and
ardently desirous of enjoying the sweets of
divine union in holy prayer, complained to the
holy Doctor that the care of the sick prevented
him from realizing the one great desire of his
heart.   "Why," replied the Saint, "do you
sigh all day long for Jesus?   Let me show you
where you are to find Him.   He is in the
infirmary, suffering and tormented there.
Hasten to wait upon Him, to relieve Him, to
give Him proofs of your tender compassion."
Yes, beloved of Jesus, you need not ask with
the Spouse in the Canticles where your Divine
Spouse is to be found; you know that He re-
poses in the infirmary.   One thing only is

necessary: that we devote ourselves to his service.

Wherefore, let the religious who are particularly charged with the care of the sick, esteem themselves happy in that office, and study to fulfil its duties with all possible perfection.

The Superior is bound to take measures to have all that concerns the wants of the sick in the best order, in the pharmacy, the kitchen, &c., and to have all that is necessary for them given to the Infirmarian promptly, and without remark. It would be a great evil if, through any distrust in Divine Providence, the expense of providing for the sick became a subject of apprehension. God would hardly fail to punish the house for such an ungenerous disposition ; perhaps, too, in its temporals.

Yet, it is not to be supposed that under pretext of caring the sick an extravagant outlay is recommended ; but it seems to us that to give to each patient what would be presented to the Superior herself, if she were visited by illness, is a sacred duty imposed by charity ; and that it marks sufficiently well the just measure to be observed in the case.

There is, however, another measure in which we can have confidence. It is that given by our Divine Lord Himself in His precept of charity : *As you would that men should do to you, do you also to them in like manner.*[1] That is to say, let us bestow on the sick the same care and affection we ourselves should be glad to receive if stretched on a bed of pain.

This rule also determines what the conduct of the sick ought to be, in order that they may not become insupportable and importunate to the Infirmarian. Let them try especially to practise patience, courage, and resignation to the Holy Will of God. St. Bernard asserts that sickness discovers the degree of perfection that each one has reached. And the Apostle St. James has written : *Patience hath a perfect work.*[2] Thus it is a sign and a measure of perfection.

The Infirmarian and the invalid ought to edify each other mutually by its practice, and so attest the degree of their perfection. And in order to do it the better and the more surely, let both keep their eyes fixed on the mirror of all patience, namely, Jesus Crucified

[1] St. Luke, vi. 31.　　[2] St. James, i. 4.

III

"Those who have charge of the Depository, habits, shoes, books, &c. should serve the Sisters without murmuring, and they ought not to delay giving what is required."

An old German proverb says that "One hand serves to wash the other," which signifies, no doubt, that while we are on earth we shall stand in need of mutual assistance; and this is the case above all in religious communities. The Apostles, themselves, chose out from among the new converts seven deacons, to whom they confided various secondary cares that were an obstacle to their apostolic zeal. But we are told expressly that the newly chosen were filled with the Holy Ghost,[1] as if to give us the consoling assurance that those lose nothing before God, who are employed in the external and apparently low and unprofitable works of a community—for holy obedience renders all such occupations grand and important. Let those to whom such charges are confided, beware of thinking that they amass fewer merits than others. On the contrary, in the exercise of fraternal charity, which is the queen of

[1] Acts, vi. 3, 4, 5.

virtues, they acquire most precious merits, besides sharing in those of the sisters whom they assist, since all is in common among the members of a religious body. The crew of a vessel have different employments, yet all sail on with equal rapidity and arrive together at the same port. Connected too with this subject is what we read in the Book of Kings, when David, after the enemy's defeat, ordered that all the warriors should receive an equal share of the spoils; as well those who had been left in care of the camp and baggage, as the others who were exposed to all the perils of battle.[1]

Even considered in themselves, the domestic functions proper to convent life should not by any means be esteemed of little value, when directed by obedience, and ennobled by the love of God and our neighbour.

St. Paul says, speaking of the angels : *Are they not all ministering spirits, sent to minister for them who shall receive the inheritance of salvation ?*[2] that is, holding to them the place of servants. And what is more, did not Mary the Queen of Angels, go to the house of her cousin,

---

[1] 1 Kings, xxx. 24.   [2] Heb. i. 14.

St. Elizabeth, for the purpose of serving her?[1]
Her Divine Son has Himself solemnly assured
us that He came *not to be ministered unto, but to
minister*.[2] How really He did this, we see in
his stooping to wash the feet of His disciples.

In the life of Blessed Hermann it is told
that he was made refectorian, and ordered at
the same time to look after all the corporal wants
of his brethren, which appointments he received
most humbly. But the exact and faithful
discharge of his duties, taking very much from
the time he was accustomed to give to contemplation, affliction and anxiety seized upon his
soul, and his thoughts frequently turned upon
the great loss that he was sustaining. In this
sad mood, going along one day through the
monastery, the ever Blessed Virgin Mother of
God, the Immaculate Mary, presented herself
before him. In few but consoling words,
she set all right. "Hermann," she said, "serve
thy brethren; and on this work alone let thy
heart be set."

Religious who have similar occupation in
their convent can profit by this recommenda-

St. Luke, i. 39, 40.   [2] St. Mark, x. 45 ; St. John, xiii. 5

tion. Let them not think it wearisome or difficult to attend to their sisters' wants; nor let them imagine those to be envied who have more leisure for retirement and prayer. To do so would be to render themselves worthy of the reproach our Lord made to Martha. Had Martha laboured at her serving silently and lovingly, she would certainly have received, not a reprimand, but well-deserved praise. I mean, if to her officious hospitality she had added the care of drawing near to the Divine Master as often as possible, and listening to his words of life.

In like manner, a thoughtless sister may forfeit much merit by her vexation and envy, by her grumbling and murmuring about her duties, instead of acquitting herself of them with humility, and in the recollected silence that so helps to sanctify labour. She may also, and very easily, become accountable for the sins of many around her, to whom her slothful, unwilling manner is a subject of scandal and bad example.

Moreover, she runs great risk of sinning against her vow of poverty, either by not paying sufficient attention to her business, and, consequently, letting matters be lost or injured through her fault, to the prejudice of the community; or by dispensing lavishly what has been confided to her care. Sisters inclined to be wasteful or extravagant should bear in mind the example given them by our Lord, when, after having, with great liberality, fed the five thousand in the desert with five barley loaves, He said to his disciples : *Gather up the fragments that remain, lest they be lost.*[1]

This teaches us, in a very striking way, that liberality may, and ought to be, combined with reasonable care and just economy. It were, indeed, much to be regretted if in this point a religious allowed herself to be surpassed in diligence and exactitude by a secular servant, who has certainly less exalted motives, and perhaps less efficient means, for conducting household affairs in an orderly and satisfactory manner.

Let all who are engaged in the domestic offices follow the directions of their Superior; by doing so they will please Almighty God, and content their sisters. Let them be affable to all, and most obliging in whatever does not

[1] St. John, vi. 12.

exceed the limits traced out for them; and when they cannot comply with a sister's wishes, their kind and charitable manner should convince her that impossibility alone prevents them.

Whoever thus valiantly exercises herself in patience and forbearance will gain many a victory over nature, and thereby acquire the merit attached to great works of penance. She will draw down on her soul torrents of graces, and her spirit will one day exult as she hears her Divine Saviour say: "Beloved soul, thou hast cared me, fed me, clothed me; yes, *thou hast been faithful over a few things; I will now place thee over many things. Enter thou into the joy of thy Lord.*"[1]

[1] St. Matt. xxv. 21.

CHAPTER XIII.

OF PEACE AND RECONCILIATION AMONGST THE SISTERS.

" Let there be neither disputes nor contentions among you. If such matters should arise, cut them short, lest anger increase to hatred, and a mote grow into a beam. For it is not alone to man that it is written : ' He who hates his brother is a murderer ;' but in the sex of man, which God created first, woman receives the same com mand."

Be angry and sin not :[1] these words of the Royal Psalmist, inspired by the Holy Spirit, indicate to us that there are two kinds of anger ; of which one is good, the other evil. The emotion of soul that we call anger is culpable only when we abandon ourselves to it at the instigation of mere passion, without following the rules of reason, or observing the measure that an enlightened zeal and just horror of sin demand.

The holy Lawgiver, Moses, is an excellent example for us in this matter. How great his indignation when, not his own, but God's

---

[1] Ps. iv. 5.

honour, had to be vindicated! And yet,
despite all the provocation he received from
his people, and all their faults, he led them
through the desert for the space of forty years,
in all mildness and patience, without quarrel
or dispute, and truly as a prince of peace. For
this reason he is called in Holy Scripture " the
meekest of men."

A generous victory over irritation and natural
impatience is no mark of weakness; far from
being so, it denotes elevation of mind and great
prudence, or, what is better, a most virtuous,
humble, and magnanimous heart. Would to
God that in religious communities this virtue
were singularly cultivated, and exercised in all
its perfections. If it be wanting, the union
and concord that are so much recommended
must cease to exist. Be assiduous, then, in
endeavouring to acquire that spirit of concilia-
tion which arrests inordinate anger and stifles
susceptibility; and to avoid, as far as possible,
all contention, observe the following advices :

1. Do not pry into the conduct of others ;
   do not judge their actions. Unless you
   watch over yourself in this point, you
   will be easily tempted to criticise, which,

sooner or later, would lead to disagreements and disputes.

2. Be indifferent, for yourself, as to what any person thinks of you. Love of humility calls for this; love of Jesus, and of Him contemned, reviled, insulted, makes it imperative. God in His goodness permits, even in religious houses, that they who are His, should have something of this kind to bear, and oftentimes, without a fault on anyone's part, He allows things to appear quite different from what they are; so that our sisters, though they suspect us, and blame us wrongfully, commit no sin thereby. If, on such occasions, we humble ourselves, not only shall we receive no hurt, but our virtue will even come forth purified from this furnace of tribulation; and all the more perfectly, in proportion as we accept judgments of this nature with tranquillity, bowing down beneath the Hand of God, without in any way disturbing the peace of our community.

Whenever a mistake, unfavourable to us,

happens to be made, we should do well to
repeat the words of St. Augustine: "Think
and say what you please of Augustine, provided
my own conscience accuse me of nothing before
God, who, one day, will be my judge." All
the saints have certainly often been rash-
judged, and have had many things falsely said
of them. But in what have they been the
worse for it? Should we not rather ask, what
benefits have they not derived from it? In
heaven their reward is eternal; their joy immense; while even on earth, biographies are
filled with their praises. Now let us fix our
eyes upon our Lord Himself during His mortal
life. Who was ever more exposed to the vain
judgments of men than He, the Holy of holies?

And He asked His disciples, saying: *Whom
do men say that the Son of man is?* [1] Oh! how
various were the opinions held about Him;
how derogatory and insulting, some of them!
There were people who said He was Elias, or
Jeremias, or one of the prophets; but others
maintained on the contrary, that He had a devil;
that He was a seducer of the people, a blas-
phemer, &c., and it was on these defaming

[1] St. Matt. xvi. 13.

charges that He was condemned to death, and fastened to an ignominious cross, between two thieves! Yet, all the time, this meek Lamb of God opened not His mouth to complain! With this example before you, Spouse of Jesus, learn whether to be alarmed and disturbed by rash judgments, or filled with inexpressible consolation at being treated like your Beloved.

3. Let all practise condescension, in order to preserve peace; their hearts should be disposed towards one another, as Abraham's was towards Lot. When strife arose between his nephew's servants and his own, he soon put an end to the rising evil; with generous condescension, he said to Lot: *Let there be no quarrel, I beseech thee, between thee and me, or between my herdsmen and thy herdsmen: for we are brethren. Behold, the whole land is before thee. . . . . if thou wilt go to the left hand, I will take the right: if thou wilt choose the right hand, I will pass to the left.*[1] Happy the soul consecrated to God, who acts according to such sentiments, and joyfully yields

[1] Gen. xiii. 8, 9.

to all her sisters, even taking the last place for herself! such a religious is an angel of peace, and her convent will be the abode of that divine virtue.

4. As far as possible let everyone abandon to God the justification of her conduct. He loves to make known the innocence of those who for love of Him, and of holy peace, refrain from justifying themselves.

5. It should be the care of each sister to attend to herself and her own employment; not to the concerns of others. Let her likewise cherish the virtue of silence; and above all things, avoid repeating lightly what she has seen or heard. It would be impossible to say how dangerous such a practice is, especially in religious communities. The remark has been made by a clever man, that it is a matter of experience, that what has been told to one person in a convent is soon known to all, on account of the perpetual state of contact that prevails. So, one sister confides the secret to another, charging her to

keep it faithfully, until it has gone the round of the house ; but always in strict confidence. Unhappily, out of such confidential communications, it is not uncommon to see many troubles and divisions spring.

All who thus openly violate the duties of their holy state may reflect to their confusion, and as a salutary warning, on these words of St. Paul : *For, whereas there is among you envying and contention, are you not carnal?*[1] that is, do you not act in a merely human manner? Yet, is not a religious bound to conduct herself in all things according to the spirit of the Lord ?

II.

" She who offends her sister by harsh or injurious words will remember to remedy the evil she has done by a prompt reparation. And, in like manner, she who has been offended ought to pardon the injury received, without entering into arguments. If both have offended each other, they ought to pardon mutually, in order to apply to prayer, which being so frequent among you, ought to be holy in proportion."

Undoubtedly, anger and injurious words

---

[1] 1 Cor. iii. 3.

should find no place in a religious community, where persons have consecrated themselves by solemn vows to a state of perfection to which duty obliges them to tend most earnestly. Nevertheless, as the enemy of our salvation, the spirit of discord, blasphemy, and envy, dares everything, even in the house of God, for the purpose of sowing cockle in the midst of good grain, and stirring up the spark of passion into a violent conflagration, there is danger to be feared, and each should do her utmost to avert it. Yes, each and all should watch over themselves, and never presume to take the smallest liberty in this point; for if one begins to give vent to ill-humour in impatient, bitter words, she will be drawn into more considerable faults. This regards not inferiors only, but likewise superiors. The latter, when obliged to reprimand, should be careful that their zeal be not excessive, or their words too strong, lest perhaps they wound, but fail to correct.

Severity is less likely to touch the heart than to render it obdurate; and a vexed spirit is incapable of receiving correction with profit, especially from one whose bitterness in reprov-

ing, shows her to be blameworthy and imperfect.

Superiors should, therefore, refrain from cor-
recting until all unusual emotion has subsided ;
and if possible, until the person in fault is herself quite calm. Under the influence of excited feeling, no one can surely determine the
just measure of a reprimand ; and it is wisely
observed by St. Ambrose that, although to a
perturbed mind all its views seem accurate, yet
there is in them generally an excess which is
extremely injurious.

Should it happen that a sister allowed herself to be so far overcome by passion and pride
as to use injurious words to another, it is clear
that she is obliged to repair the pain and offence
she has given by retracting and asking pardon.
In case the fault were public, the reparation
should be so too; otherwise the consequences
might be fatal to peace and fraternal union.

On her side the person who has been offended
should consider the occasion a precious one for
humbling herself, and reaping the advantages
already spoken of ; and she should be the more
ready to pardon fully when a reparation has
been made.

When so much is required of the children of the world, as is contained in the words of our divine Lord: *Love your enemies : do good to them that hate you,*[1] how strong must the obligation be that binds a religious not to let aversion or displeasure appear in consequence of any offence she may have received. And this holds good, not once, or seven times, as St. Peter supposed, but even seventy times seven ; that is an indefinite number of times—in one word, always.

How forcibly the Lord's prayer recalls this obligation : *Forgive us our trespasses as we forgive them that trespass against us ;*[2] and those other words of our Heavenly Master: *But if you will not forgive men, neither will your Father forgive you your offences.*[3]

III.

"Now that sister is so much the more to be esteemed, who being often tempted to vivacity and anger is prompt in asking pardon, than is another who not being so easily moved, is unwilling to make an apology. And she who will not pardon should not hope to be heard in prayer, and she who is unwilling to ask pardon may believe that in vain and uselessly is she in the monastery, though not

---

[1] St. Matt. v. 44.   [2] St. Matt. vi. 12.
[3] St. Matt. vi. 15.

expelled thence. Refrain, then, from all rude words towards each other, and if any such escape your lips delay not to apply a remedy to the wounds with that very same tongue which has caused them.

It is easy to conclude from all that has been said, that it is a certain sign of the presence of the Spirit of God in a Religious, when she lives among her sisters without wounding charity; neither giving nor taking offence, simple and innocent as the dove, yet with the prudence of the serpent, avoiding all that might be distasteful to others. Nor should she forfeit her privilege, though by some inconsiderate act she were occasionally to fail, provided she try by a prompt reparation, to restore perfect harmony and order. But a religious who should treat her sisters rudely, and seek no pardon, nor even evince regret by the humility of her manner, or by a few amiable words, or some excuse or explanation, as the matter might require, would be unworthy of her name, and of the holy habit that she wears.

The Superior is bound to use her authority with such a person, to impose the necessary penance, and insist on her amendment. How devoted soever to prayer and corporal mortification that religious might be, still so long as she neglects to overcome herself and practise charity, she would be in the eyes of God, as the Apostle writes: *but, as a sounding brass, and a tinkling cymbal.*[1] It is principally to this interior mortification that we are to apply these words of our Lord: *The kingdom of heaven suffereth violence.*[2] Let a man endure even martyrdom, if he harbour enmity in his heart, hell must be his portion, according to what St. John writes: *If any man say, I love God and hateth his brother; he is a liar;*[3] and charity is not in him.

As a powerful encouragement in this point, we ought to keep before our minds the example of the saints, whose chief kindness was displayed towards those from whom they had received most evil. They acted thus because they loved their Divine Master, and ardently desired to imitate Him.

Let us also remember how the Apostles, after the descent of the Holy Ghost, rejoiced to suffer opprobrium for the name of Jesus; and let us thank God that His wise providence has ordained

[1] 1 Cor. xiii. 1. [2] St. Matt. xi. 12.
[3] 1 Ep. St. John, iv. 20.

for us occasions of becoming participators in the same holy joy and its merits.

Yes, Spouse of Christ, if you are really what your name declares, you must not allow yourself to be overcome by evil; but rather you will overcome evil by good, *that you may be the child of your Father who is in heaven.*[1]

Suffer with patience, considering what precious treasures the religious life opens to you, and say with Job: *If we have received good things at the hand of God, why should we not receive evil?*[2] Does not everything that happens turn to the good of our souls, if we only wish it?

It is true that this does not always seem clear to us. We may compare the plan of God's grace to some exquisitely flowered tissue. Look to the wrong side: no pattern is apparent; the threads all run in a confused, irregular fashion. But turn the stuff, hold it in the proper light, and all the richness, ingenuity, and beauty of the design are made evident. Thus, at times the secret dispositions of God, judged by our sense, seem to want consecutiveness, connection, and order; but the judgments of the Lord

[1] St. Matt. v. 45.   [2] Job, i. 10.

will one day unveil what is hidden from us now.

Then we shall see the verification of the words of the Apostle : *To them that love God all things work together unto good.*[1] What a consolation for those who have hard trials to endure, to reflect on this oracle of the Holy Ghost ! For those who hope patiently in Him, the Lord will, some day, draw the greatest good from all the evil that is happening to them. As to the religious state, it is just that those who are in possession of the many treasures of grace attached to it, should, at the same time, have something to suffer. And it would be very surprising if a soul, after devoting herself wholly to the imitation of Jesus Christ, should refuse to share in his Cross and its ignominy.

Conclude, then, to follow the counsel of the Prophet, who says : *In silence and in hope shall your strength be ;*[2] and trust sweetly in the Lord, who solemnly assures us of his compassionate care, saying : *Can a woman forget her infant, so as not to have pity on the son of her womb ? and if she should forget, yet will not I forget thee.*[3]

---

[1] Rom. viii. 28.   [2] Isaias, xxx. 15.   [3] Isaias, xlix. 15.

IV.

"When the duty of your office obliges you to use severe expressions, either for the instruction or correction of those confided to you, in case you exceed the exact bounds of moderation, you are not to ask pardon for so doing; because thus, under a pretext of humility, you may diminish your authority, and become less useful in conducting those persons. Still, you ought to ask pardon from God, the common Lord and Master of all, who well knows how tenderly you love that soul, whom you have reprehended with perhaps more bitterness than necessary. It is a spiritual, not a sensible love, which should exist between you."

It is most certain that human nature in general is more easily led by kindness than by rigour; therefore, Superiors, following the example of our Lord, whose place they hold, should study to govern with mildness rather than with severity. Instead of exact justice, we find that indulgence, mercy, and clemency are the chief characteristics of the way by which God's grace conducts man to his high destination. We know it by our own experience; for, alas! what should have been our fate had not divine mercy spared us, and brought us into holy religion? But God's just judgments, too, are brought into action when nothing else will awaken man from his sleep of sin, and excite him to sincere repentance and amendment.

Our Divine Saviour Himself gives us in the Gospel most striking examples of patience, sweetness, and mildness; yet He also employed severe reprimands in cases of obstinate guilt or great negligence. He teaches us a lesson in the parable of the Good Samaritan. This generous stranger, taking compassion on the man who fell among robbers, poured into his wounds not only oil, but wine, to show us that we must mingle rigour with gentleness in our treatment of others, especially when their conduct merits reproof.

Every Superior is obliged to pursue this wise method; she should even do herself violence in order to carry it out faithfully; for nature is prone to excess, whether of mildness or its contrary. Let her diligently make her examen on this important point, and often beg light to act with charity and prudence, so that she may be neither too lenient nor too rigorous. She would do well to make choice of a sister to observe her in this respect, and to remind her when she fails. Let her often say to God, with holy David: *From my hidden sins, O Lord,*

13

*deliver me, and from the sins of others save thy
servant.*[1]   That is, from sins occasioned by
neglect or undue severity.

If she has failed so as to wound the reputation
of one of her sisters, she owes her a becoming
reparation, made, however, in such a way that
the sister may have no idea of resisting another
time; and made, moreover, without compromis-
ing her authority or the dignity of her office,
which she must always endeavour to maintain.

As to the person unjustly censured, she
should beware of wishing for any reparation
from her Superior; she has cause only for joy
at having got to suffer something that may
liken her, even remotely, to Jesus outraged and
despised.   Should she have some matter of
consequence to allege in her own justification,
she ought, in the first place, to recommend it
fervently to God in prayer, and then to give
her explanation modestly and respectfully to her
Superior, remembering that it is our Lord
Himself who directs her by his representative;
and that though He may permit her, as it
would seem, through some mistake, to be unde-
servedly penanced, He will finally make all
conduce to the good of her soul.

We often read in the "Lives of the Saints" how God, by such means as these, purified the virtues of his servants, and augmented their merits, in order to remunerate them the more richly in His kingdom of eternal glory. Superior and inferior will one day stand before Christ's tribunal. May the account that they shall then render—one of her maternal solicitude, the other of her patient and humble submission—be for their eternal happiness.

CHAPTER XIV.

OF OBEDIENCE AND THE OBSERVANCE OF RULE.

" Obey your Mother Superior as your mother, rendering unto her all due honour, lest God might be offended ; and pay yet more honour to the Father Superior, who has charge of all."

Moses and Aaron were appointed by God as leaders over the people of Israel. When, therefore, this people began to be discontented with them, Moses said : *The Lord hath heard your murmuring ; but what are we that you*

mutter against us? He was right; for it was
the Lord who had placed them at the head of
their nation, and clothed them with His own
power.

Samuel made a similar response. The
Israelites grew weary of him, and asked for a
king. Samuel said to them: It is not me
whom you have rejected, but it is the Lord,
that He should not reign over you. Jesus
Christ solemnly assures us that whoever resists
Superiors resists Himself, *He who heareth you,*
heareth me; and he who despiseth you, despiseth
me.[1] And He insists still more strongly on this
truth, which is of special importance in the
religious state, in these words of his Apostle :
There is no power but from God . . . therefore
he that resisteth the power, resisteth the ordinance
of God.[2]

But what is to be said of the obedience which
religious solemnly vow, and by which they give
themselves up entirely to the guidance of God,
through the direction of Superiors. It is
rightly named the soul of the religious state,
for when it flourishes all is prosperous; but if
it decline, the ship of religion itself swerves

[1] St. Luke, x. 16   [2] Rom. xiii. 1, 2.

from its true course, and is wrecked in consequence.

As long as Simon Machabeus dwelt in the land, there was peace and quiet; Simon signifies obedience. Wherever this virtue abides, order, tranquillity, and peace are to be found; but let it disappear, and disorder, dissension, and trouble take its place. How, in the midst of such enemies, could a religious Order continue to subsist?

Do thoughts and considerations of this nature ever enter the minds of those religious who, notwithstanding their holy vow of obedience, are as wedded to their own opinion as if their vow had been of an opposite kind, namely, to do their own will, instead of the will of those over them? Or can they be well convinced of the sacredness of their obligations, who render mere external obedience, under constraint, and unaccompanied by submission of judgment? We may entertain the same doubt of persons, who, instead of looking on their Superior as God's representative, criticise her, and judge of her by her natural qualities and capacity, forgetting that, for them, she is the exponent of God's will, and that in obeying her they ought to commit themselves blindly to His Providence. Is it not easy for this all-wise and all-powerful Father to procure the accomplishment of His ever holy and adorable will; and if need be, by a thousand unforeseen circumstances, to overcome the resistance of Superiors? And can He not thus, by obedience, conduct us in humility, faith, confidence, and love, to our supreme end.

We may learn from all this how little of the virtue of obedience those religious possess, who discuss and judge the orders of Superiors according to human views. They never say to themselves: " Who knows the secret designs of God in this matter, or whether He may permit such and such a thing to happen, for reasons unthought of by man?" And yet, experience proves that affairs sometimes take a different course, and arrive at quite an opposite turn, to that on which human foresight had calculated.

Religious, especially, must often have realized the advantages accruing from the regulations of Superiors, and have got convinced that things would have gone on very badly, if they themselves had had their way.

It is altogether opposed to perfect obedience for a religious, as soon as she has received some order, to go to one of her sisters and ask her opinion thereupon. Disagreements, confusion, and disrespect to Superiors are the necessary consequences of such conduct. St. Bernard says, that true obedience never questions or examines much; but where there is no manifest sin in the command, it obeys promptly and perseveringly; and honours the Will of God, not that of man, in the voice, or at the beck of the Superior.

You should not seek, as some do, when the Superior gives an order, to find out reasons and ways for bringing it into accordance with your own will. Whoever acts so, and obtains her desire, is not obeying her Superior; it is the Superior who obeys her. Surely such obedience is no virtue. St. Bernard calls it "a cloak and a veil for malice." It is a reversing of the order of salvation; a revoking of the sacrifice of self-will, so solemnly made to God by the vow of obedience. Oh! that those who presume to transgress in this matter would remember the warnings of the Spirit of God, in the Sacred Text: *If thou hast vowed anything to the Lord, defer not to pay it, for an unfaithful*

*promise displeaseth Him ; and it is much better
not to vow, than after a vow not to perform the
things promised.*[1]

Elsewhere we read the still stronger sen-
tence : *Obedience is better than sacrifice.*[2] In fact,
Holy Scripture contains the most terrifying
threats on this subject, and indignant protests
against the very best works, when performed
through self-will, and contrary to holy obedience.

In the Book of Ecclesiastes we read, that
neither fasts nor sacrifices are acceptable to God
if obedience do not sanction them. And our
Blessed Saviour protests that He will not ac-
knowledge as His own, but rather will condemn
many who shall have cast out devils, and
wrought miracles in His name, but who in doing
these things followed their own will, not the
will of His Heavenly Father.

How often, on the other hand, has not the
Lord God proved, by miraculous effects, the
pleasure that He takes in perfect obedience. The
"Lives of the Saints," and the Annals of different
Orders, are filled with marvellous instances.

---

[1] Eccles. v. 4.   [2] 1 Kings, xv 22.

Thus, St. Maur walked upon the waters, without sinking, at a word from his Superior. Among the Fathers of the Desert, there was another Superior who ordered one of his disciples to catch a lioness, and bring her to him; he was obeyed directly. Another young monk at the call of obedience, took and carried to some distance, an enormous rock that several men could not lift.

Such miracles attest the extreme complacency which Almighty God takes in the generous exercise of holy obedience. Let each one then study to excel in this sublime virtue, and endeavour to make it a constant and unfailing habit, by her prompt, full, and joyful submission to the orders of Superiors, as well as by her fidelity to the Rules, Constitutions, and daily regular observances.

As to the orders of Superiors, perfection consists in accomplishing them promptly and fully; and this, not only when something is commanded in virtue of obedience, but even when the order is expressed merely by a sign. There is no exception, unless what is enjoined us be sinful, or contrary to the Rules and discipline of the Order; for in such a case a Superior would abuse her charge, and we should declare to her in all humility and sincerity that conscience forbade us to obey. Yet, when delay is possible, the Confessor ought to be consulted, as he, from his priestly office, can best judge whether what has been ordered is sinful, or opposed to our holy Rule.

In all other circumstances the most prompt and punctual obedience is due to every wish of the Superior, though manifested only by a simple sign ; and always an exact and generous observance of everything prescribed by our Rules is to be lovingly cultivated. God has very often miraculously shown that the sacrifice of obedience was more acceptable to Him than prayers and penances.

We shall add, in conclusion and confirmation of what we have said of the sanctity and gravity of the obligation contracted by the vow of obedience, those terrible words from the first Book of Kings, where there is question of the disobedience of Saul : *It is like the sin of witchcraft to rebel, and like the crime of idolatry to refuse to obey.*[1] A frightful sentence, yet, most true !

[1] 1 Kings, xv. 23.

For in what, properly speaking, does the malice of magic and idolatry consist?

Magic attributes supreme science to itself, by presuming to predict what God alone can know.

Idolatry consists in preferring the creature to the Creator, and paying to it divine honour; both these vices lead to perdition.

This is precisely what disobedience does. The disobedient soul thinks she knows better what she ought to do than God Himself, who informs her of His will through her Superior. She incurs the guilt of magic by supposing that if events come to pass according to her ordering, all will be for the best.

Again, the disobedient religious prefers herself to her Superior, and consequently to the authority of God; she renders to her self-love the honour due to God alone, and thus becomes guilty of the sin of idolatry, turning away from her Lord to worship the spirit of pride, the enemy of our salvation—the demon.

Oh, my very dear Sisters! if we consider all this, shall we wonder at Blessed Egidius of the Order of Friars minors, for saying that "she who is trying to live according to her own will in a convent, is going straight to hell." " Be ashamed, proud souls," exclaims St. Bernard, " you, who are but dust and ashes, God abases Himself, and you seek elevation ; God submits to man in the person of Mary and Joseph, while you wish to rule others, and prefer yourselves to God !"

Ah ! how could an indocile religious flatter herself that she was the Spouse of Christ, of whom it is written : *He humbled Himself, becoming obedient unto death, even to the death of the Cross.*[1] Amen.

CHAPTER XV.

OF THE OFFICE OF MOTHER SUPERIOR.

" In order to have all these points observed, and that through neglect matters may not be allowed to go on without correction and amendment, the Mother Superior should be vigilant ; and if any circumstance occur which lies beyond her power or her capacity, she may consult with the Father Superior, who has the superintendence of the monastery."

WHEN the Lord God had given His people the Law, written on two tables of stone, Moses assembled the ancients, and repeated all that he

[1] Phil. ii. 8.

had been ordered to announce to them; and the people answered: "We will execute all that God has pronounced." Yet they soon forgot the marvellous and multiplied graces they had received from Him, together with the alliance made between them; and the anger of the Lord was manifested in fearful chastisements and scourges.

All this is realised in the religious souls, who, notwithstanding the numberless graces that accompany their holy vocation, and after uttering their solemn vows, forget in a manner, this divine alliance, and instead of making continual progress in perfection sink, every day deeper, into tepidity and sloth. Externally they seem still to be religious; but alas! *how is the gold become dim?*[1] Virtue is sadly obscured in their hearts. It is the duty of a Superior to do all that she can to prevent so great a misfortune befalling any soul under her care.

Let her, in the first place, see that all read, and diligently and attentively meditate, on the Rules and Constitutions, in order that they may have them always present to their memory.

---

[1] Lam. iv. 1.

But this is not sufficient. It is written in St. James: *For if a man be a hearer of the word, and not a doer, he shall be compared to a man beholding his own countenance in a glass. For he beheld himself and went his way, and presently forget what manner of man he was.*[1] Not those who only hear the word, but those who accomplish it will be happy.

The Superior must be solicitous for the observance of the Rules and Constitutions; she should endeavour by her vigilance and her example, to ensure having all her sisters, ' ' doers of the word ; " and, as has been already said, she will exhort and penance transgressors. *Son of Man,* said the Lord to Ezechiel, *I have made thee a watchman to the house of Israel, and thou shalt hear the word out of my mouth, and shall tell it them from me. If, when I say to the wicked : Thou shalt surely die ; thou declare it not to him, nor speak to him that he may be converted from his wicked way and live : the same wicked man shall die in his iniquity, but I will require his blood at thy hand.*[2]

Yes, Mother Superior, those words of the

---

[1] St. James, i. 23, 24.   [2] Ezech. iii. 17, 18.

Lord are addressed to you; God has established you the guardian of His house! Announce His word and His will according to the holy Rule and observances of the Order; instruct, exhort, encourage your daughters, in order that they may maintain themselves in the first fervour of their holy profession, or recover it, if lost; and then advance and grow strong in all virtue. If you neglect this duty, and that any of them fall into tepidity through your fault, she, it is true, will be judged according to her works; but you also will be called to a severe account. And if one were lost for ever through your neglect of duty, God would hold you answerable for that soul.

How terrifying those words! Reflected on very seriously they would help one to understand how full of responsibility is the charge of a Superior; and would reanimate the determination of Superiors to keep their conscience clear before God, by the most zealous solicitude for the salvation of those confided to their care.

II.

"As to the Mother Superior, let her not esteem herself happy in having the power of governing or commanding, but rather in being able to serve the Sisters with charity."

From all that has been said hitherto, it follows clearly that there is little reason to desire the office of Superior, charged as it is with responsibility, and leading to a judgment so severe. The Holy Spirit says expressly: *A most severe judgment shall be for them that rule.*[1]

No doubt, the elevated post might seem desirable, considering only appearances; for a Superior seems more free and more honoured than those who are subject to her jurisdiction; but in reality, there is no one under heavier obligations, since she has to answer for everything that passes in her Convent, in so far as matters depend on her vigilance.

Notwithstanding this, it is certain that a Superior ought not to trouble herself beyond what is just and necessary, when she has been raised to her office at the call, and by the Will

[1] Wis. vi. 6.

of God; but she needs to tremble if she has opened the way to it for herself, and if she has been more desirous of enjoying its privileges, than anxious to fulfil its duties. Ah! let her imagine the cry of despair that will break forth from, perhaps, many souls through all eternity. "Had I not been a Superior, I should not now be damned!"

However, as Superiors are indispensably necessary, and as their charge is meritorious in proportion to its pains and difficulties; provided always that it has been undertaken for God, and that it is borne in union with Him; all engaged in it should examine themselves on the following points:

1. A Superior may ask herself whether she has been raised to her office according to her own wish, or against it. The great Apostle says: *Neither doth any man take the honour to himself, but he that is called by God.*[1]

2. Let her consider with what dispositions she accepted the charge imposed on her. Even founders of Religious Orders have

---

[1] Heb. v. 4.

refused, with great humility, to be Superiors in the same; or if constrained to submit, through fear of resisting the known Will of God, they prepared for their important and responsible functions, by the spiritual exercises, solitude, prayer, fasting, and many austerities. They had at heart this word of the Lord Jesus: *Whoever entereth not by me, the same is a thief and a robber.*[1]

3. Let her ask herself how she has discharged her obligations up to the present time, whether it has been in a manner that tended to her own salvation, and that of all who are under her care. To effect this, it is necessary that she render her life so faithful a copy of her holy Rule as to be to all her sisters what a mirror is to an apartment. Inferiors look to the example of those over them, and are guided more by what they see, than by what they hear. A mirror to be useful must be clear and bright; if covered with dust

[1] St. John, xi. 1.

and dirt, how can it serve to make us acquainted with our defects?

4. Finally, she should reflect whether the dignity of her office has produced in her an increase of humility, conformably to this injunction of our Blessed Lord: *He that is greatest among you, shall be your servant.*[1] By this sign especially, a Superior is known to have been elected by a true vocation to her important charge; and it is a great proof that she fulfils her duties in the spirit of that vocation, when she feels humbled at the thought of her unworthiness, and of the responsibility that weighs upon her in that post of honour. Guided by this spirit she will govern her Community with true charity, and avoid the extremes of indulgence and severity. She will employ her authority for the benefit and consolation of her daughters; her heavy burden will be made light, and will become a rich source of merit and reward; while her elevated position, in-

[1] St. Matt. xxiii. 11.

stead of being the occasion of falls, will
be for her as Jacob's ladder, by which
she may ascend to Heaven.   Amen.

III.

" Let her precede you in all honour before the world ;
but before God let her be humbly submissive at your feet,
and offer to all the example of good works. Let her
correct disturbers, console the timid, support and embrace
the infirm, and let her be patient towards all, applying correction willingly, yet with dread. Let her desire rather
to be loved than feared by you, though both are necessary ;
and she should ever remember that she will have an
account to render to God of you all."

Honour to whom honour is due.[1]   These words
possess additional force and importance when
the spiritual good of a Community, as in the
Religious Orders, depends on their observance.

It is right and necessary that the Superiors
should be treated with the greatest honour ; because on one side, the authority of God, which
is the motive of our obedience, shines forth pre-
eminently in the Heads of Religious Houses ;

---

[1] Rom. xiii. 7.

and on the other, subjects are bound to have an affectionate zeal for this sacred duty, of which they are so constantly reminded in their Rules and Constitutions.

The maintenance of discipline in the Order, depends materially on the esteem and respect entertained and expressed for those who are in authority. So that it would be very false humility in a Superior to lower herself, or allow her daughters to treat her with disrespect. She may be really humble, and yet careful to preserve intact all the honour and influence attached to her charge.

In order to succeed in this, it is necessary for her to regulate her conduct so perfectly, that all in her may inspire her sisters with truly filial deference. Indeed little more is wanted, than that she should be, as we have already said, a mirror and model of religious observance. An opposition between her teaching and her practice, would be self-condemnation from her own lips, and would greatly lessen the consideration in which she ought to be held. But, to instruct by example, rather than words, confirms authority and ensures respect and obedience.

The example of Gedeon is admirably suited to our subject. He marched against the Madianites with three hundred men, and before the battle he said to these: *What you shall see me do, do you the same.*[1] Then, having taken a trumpet, he sounded it, and broke the pitcher that he held in his left hand, and in which a lamp was concealed. The sound of the trumpet is the voice of the Superior, crying out like St. Paul to the Corinthians: *Be ye followers of me, as I also am of Christ.*[2] Thus, by word and example, she precedes her community. The breaking of the pitcher signifies humility, which is to accompany all that she says and does, in order that her virtue may shine as a lamp, and that she and her spiritual daughters may gain victories over the Madianites, that is, the enemies of their souls ; and over everything opposed to the holy customs of their Order. In a similar spirit, St. Paul wrote to his beloved disciple, Timothy : *Be thou an example to the faithful, in word, in conversation, in charity, in faith, in chastity. . . . For in doing this, thou shalt both save thyself, and them that hear thee.*[3]

---

[1] Judges, vii. 17, 20. [2] 1 Cor. iv. 16. [3] 1 Tim. iv. 12 16.

The Superior should also endeavour to gain the affection of the Sisters, by a truly maternal interest in all that concerns them, and to inspire them with great confidence, so that in all their troubles, they may recur to her frankly and freely.

Some of them may be tormented with sadness and apprehension, imagining they had never made a good confession; some will suffer violent temptations; thoughts against faith, and doubts of the mercy of God will assail others; and some, in short, may find the strictness of religious discipline very trying to nature.

With regard to the pusillanimous, St. Bernard's advice to the Superior is as follows : "If you observe that one of yours is afflicted and dejected, remember that you are her mother, and that you are bound to console her by your advice and instruction, pointing out to her the stratagems of the enemy, and how he tries, by his perplexing and harassing deceits, to ruin those whom he cannot tempt to forsake the way of salvation."

Let her then be ready to give timorous souls such explanations and assurances as are proper to allay fear, according to the different sources

from which it springs. For instance, a sister
tormented with uneasiness about the validity of
her confessions—no uncommon thing—should
be told that God does not require impossibilities.
He wills us to cast ourselves with confidence
into the arms of His divine mercy, after we have
taken reasonable care to make our confession
well ; and He is much more honoured by this
humility and filial abandonment, than He could
be by our confidence, if we knew, beyond all
doubt, that our sins were pardoned.

It is for the purpose of exercising and
strengthening us in the two fundamental virtues
of the Christian life, humility and confidence,
that God permits us to feel some uneasiness
concerning the state of our conscience ; it is a
safeguard against the great perils of self-esteem
and vanity. *Blessed is the man that feareth the
Lord*,' says the Holy Spirit. It should also be
remarked that contrition consists not so much
in tears or sensible sorrow as in the will that
detests sin, and shuns relapses. When a soul
has to battle with violent temptations, the
Superior should recall to her mind the exhortation of the Spirit of God, addressed to her by

¹ Ps. cxi. 1.

the mouth of Solomon : *My child, when thou comest to the service of God, ... prepare thy soul for temptation.*[1] Is it not natural that the evil spirit should employ all his efforts to oppose those who are resolved on giving themselves without reserve to God ? " Be assured, my brethren," says St. Augustine, "that the demon persecutes the good and the devout. As to his friends, that is those who do his will, not only does he not tempt them, but he even makes use of them to trouble pious and holy souls."

The sister may be encouraged by such considerations as these ; she can also be led to see that it is solely for her perfection God allows her to be so severely tried ; and in order that she may better know her own frailty ; that she may practise heroic acts of of abnegation ; and press forward with greater fervour and zeal in the road of the opposite virtues ; just as the barking cry of the hounds causes the hunted stag to run more swiftly over the hills and mountains.

If we hasten with all our might the Lord will not permit these dogs of temptation to

---

[1] Ecclus. ii. 1.

overtake and wound us. *God is faithful*, says St. Paul, *and will make with temptation issue, that you may be able to bear it.*[1] And in the soul that perseveres in the midst of trial, are verified these words of the Divine Spirit: *Because thou wast acceptable to God, it was necessary that temptation should prove thee.*[2] Let her beware of thinking that her trials are too violent, or beyond her strength; for as faith and reason teach, *God will not permit her to be tempted beyond that which she is able to bear.*[3]

If a sister is tempted against faith, the Superior should engage her to despise both the enemy of salvation and his lying suggestions.

What surpassing folly indeed, to doubt the truth of our holy faith, after the nineteen centuries during which it has borne such abundant fruits in the Church of God! It would be less insane to doubt whether the sun gives light at noon; for the proofs of our divine religion are more credible, than is any natural fact which the whole world looks on as incontrovertible.

Let the sisters be reminded of the choir of

---

[1] 1 Cor. x. 13. [2] Tobias, xii. 13. [3] 1 Cor. x. 13.

Martyrs, millions in number; of the holy Pontiffs, Confessors, and Virgins, whose faith brought them to such sublime perfection ; and who in return, rendered to it a testimony so bright and glorious, as only those who have nearly lost their reason can fail to understand. By these, and similar recollections, this afflicted soul will be brought to despise her doubts.

As to one who might be tempted to lose heart under the difficulties of religious observance, let the Superior speak to her of the merit of the life to which she has been called; of the "Royal Way of the Cross," of the magnificent reward laid up for us in Heaven, if here below we suffer with our Jesus, and for Him ; and remind her of what St. Paul says : *that all the sufferings of this time are not to be compared with the glory to come that shall be revealed in us.*[1] The crown of life is for the victorious only, and if our holy Rules sometimes weigh heavily, the children of the world are not less burdened by the exigences of their state ; nay, frequently, their burden is much more unbearable.

But in order that the sisters may derive from

---

[1] Rom. viii. 18.

the words of their Superior, the consolation she would fain impart, it is above all things necessary that she should possess their confidence, and be loved by them. Therefore, let her manifest the most maternal solicitude, not merely for a few, but for all. To make distinctions would be harmful. St. Paul excepts no one when he says : *Brethren, if any one be overtaken in a fault, instruct him in the spirit of meekness, considering thyself, lest thou also be tempted.*

It is indispensable for a Superior to resist the attacks of impatience and vexation, to which the numerous cares and obligations of her position expose her ; especially when she has been a long time in office. Let her consider Jesus in His quality of victim, and persuade herself that as she holds the place of Christ, it is fitting that she should be immolated with Him. If, acting on such motives, says St. Bonaventure, a Superior always preserves a modest dignity of manner combined with the courtesy that becomes a religious, answering her sisters kindly, giving no sign of impatience by look, voice, or gesture ; if she tries to live in peace with all, not seeking satisfaction for any personal

[1] Gal. vi. 1.

wrong, or diminishing her good offices towards those who have offended her, she will find favour with God, receive the approbation of her fellow-mortals, and, aided by the divine blessing, she will guide her spiritual flock to their very great advantage. How troublesome soever to nature this line of conduct may seem at first, it will in time become more easy; and she will multiply her merits in proportion as she shall overcome greater difficulties.

She would do well to consider how exactly the angel guardians acquit themselves of their charge. Their watchful charity is never at fault; yet, when souls do not profit by it, they have no desire to relinquish the care of them, and their peace and felicity in God's sight remains unruffled. A Superior ought often to recommend herself to the Holy Angels of her sisters, that they may obtain for her the necessary grace to direct those souls for whose salvation the heavenly spirits and she are jointly charged to watch.

St. Gregory the Great advises a Superior, who is discouraged at the little fruit her exertions produce, to reflect on some of her own imperfections, which she has been long labouring to correct and as yet without the desired success. She should, therefore, never despair of others, nor be inclined to doubt of their good will. Many excellent things, too, are done without making any show; although a tree is really growing there is no perceptible increase in its dimensions for some time; and how little common sense it would argue in a gardener who should think it not worth his care on that account. God will not judge a Superior by the fruit of her labours, but by the zeal and devotedness which animated them. She must not then be unreasonably anxious. And moreover, she should understand well, that all that is right and good in itself is not always expedient; that something must be left to time and to the action of God's sweet Providence, which regulates the progressive development of virtue in souls.

Accordingly, the Superior has to adapt herself to persons and circumstances; making herself all to all, as she shall be enlightened and drawn by the Holy Ghost. If He replenish her soul with truth, strength, and consolation, she will be able to decide in particular cases, as our Lord would have her do; and she will govern in the spirit of charity, not in the spirit of fear and rigour.

Let her conduct be such that her sisters may submit to her with filial respect and entire esteem. And above all things, let her love them ; for then they will gladly follow both her advice and her example, since *Charity, is the bond of perfection.*[1] Thus she will one day be able *to render a joyful account to Jesus Christ of the souls He had confided to her.*[2] But that Superiors and subjects may mutually aid and support each other on the road to heaven they should fervently comply with the advice of the Apostle, St. James : *Pray one for another, that you may be saved.*[3]

IV.

"In obeying her have compassion, not alone on yourselves, but also on her, who among you is exposed to a danger so much the more to be apprehended, as her charge is the more eminent. May God give you grace to observe all these points with charity, loving the spiritual beauty of virtues, and exhaling by your holy conversation a good odour in Jesus Christ."

From all that has been said in these pages of Superiority, it is clear that the charge is much

[1] Col. iii. 14.   [2] Heb. xiii. 17.   [3] St. James, v. 16.

more to be dreaded than coveted. The Superior has, in some sort, as many souls as there are members in her Community; consequently, as St. Gregory remarks, so many burdens to carry. And it remains to be said that all distinction accorded us by our equals, especially when it abandons us to our own will, is often hurtful to the holiest souls. While he was only a subject David sinned not; but being king, and become his own master, great was his fall. Some pious writers, considering the touching picture of Jesus weeping over Jerusalem on the day of His earthly triumph, conclude that all worldly elevation, in the view that God takes of it, far from being desirable, should be a subject of affliction. Every sister ought, therefore, to endeavour by all means in her power, to lighten her Superior's burden, by carrying out her orders and wishes with a great zeal for her own perfection, according to the spirit of her Order; and by being careful not to grieve the heart of her mother, or to add to the load that weighs upon her, by any carelessness or indocility.

May God preserve you all from such a misfortune! St. Ignatius assures us that if the Angels could weep, they would shed bitter tears over a soul fallen away from fervour, and grown cool in the practice of virtue.

Would to God that there were fewer than there are, who, after setting out with zeal, and being a consolation to Superiors, realize in the end the complaint which the Lord makes by the mouth of Jeremias : *Thou hast broken my yoke ; thou hast burst my bands, and thou saidest : " I will not serve."*[1]

The sweet yoke of the Lord is the yoke of obedience, and the faithful observance of the holy Vows, Rules, and Constitutions, to which the Spouse of Jesus has solemnly bound herself. May we be permitted now to ask whether each soul, consecrated to God, practises them with the requisite exactitude and fidelity?

Alas! how many there are, who, during their time of probation in the Novitiate, were more fervent and punctual than they have been since their holy profession! And what an inconceivable abuse of the reason and the will, to be more fervent and exact in performing that to which no promise binds, than in fulfilling the same after having vowed and sworn fidelity!

---

[1] Jer. ii. 20.

The soul that errs so greatly, must completely forget the warning of the Holy Spirit as declared by the Wise Man: *If thou hast vowed anything to God, defer not to pay it, for an unfaithful promise displeaseth Him.*[1]

Of what use can it be to a soul to have entered the religious state, unless she continue to the end faithful to her obligations? An order in which the Rule is no longer in vigour, sadly verifies the words of the Royal Prophet: *Thou hast broken down the hedge thereof: so that all they who pass by the way do pluck it.*[2]

God revealed to blessed Gerard of the Cistercian Order, as St. Bernard affirms, that Religious who observe their Rule, are not only in no danger of damnation, but that they will even rank among the holy martyrs in heaven. Where, on the contrary, in the abode of eternal despair, will be the place of those who violate their vows, despise their Rules and Constitutions, and transgress them in word and action?

It is really incomprehensible that Religious do not consider all this as they ought; and equally

---

[1] Eccles. v. 3.   [2] Ps. lxxix. 13.

so, that sometimes after the lapse of years, they come to find the exercises of their state a pain to them, instead of experiencing the facility in their performance, which results from persevering practice in any occupation. It is true that there are souls who for a long time have ceased to make progress; they showed a greater aptitude for virtue during their Novitiate than now, when they should have arrived at perfection.

Ah! that these words of the Saviour would sink into their hearts: *I have somewhat against thee, because thou hast left thy first charity.*[1] She who desires to escape this reproach, and its fatal consequences, should frequently excite herself to fervour; should recommence every day, and renew herself in spirit, in order that at the hour when the Lord shall come, she may be ready, as a Wise Virgin, to enter with Him, the Divine Bridegroom, into the nuptial hall, where we all hope to receive one day an ineffable recompense, and to find our portion in the inheritance of the Saints. Amen.

[1] Apoc. ii. 4.

V.

"But in order that you may behold yourselves in this Rule, as it were in a mirror, it will be read for you once every week, fearing that through forgetfulness you might neglect some point. If you find that you do all that is here prescribed, render thanksgiving to God, from whom all good comes. But if some one of you perceives that she has failed in any matter, let her repent of what is past, and take better care for the future, praying to God that her fault may be forgiven, and that she may not be led into temptation."

Every daughter of St. Augustine who, according to her vocation, aspires to the perfection of virtue, and wishes to attain the sanctity proper to her state, should endeavour to acquire a perfect knowledge of the spirit of her holy Rule, the explanation of which has now been given. This will enable her to follow her vocation in security, without ever wandering from the road ; and in the end, to accomplish all the designs of God upon her soul. Let all that has been said on her holy Rule, be to her as a mirror, in which, viewing herself. she may discover her defects to correct them. Let her impress on her memory and heart all that is contained in this book, for *he that keepeth the*

Commandment, keepeth his own soul,[1] as the Holy Spirit assures us, in the Book of Proverbs. She should also bear in mind the exhortation of the Great Apostle : *Let him that standeth take heed lest he fall.*[2] But if he has fallen, let him not despair, but invoke with great confidence the Mercy of God, rise generously, and show himself to be the conqueror of Satan. That is to say, she who while meditating her holy Rule and this commentary, receives from her conscience the testimony that she walks according to the spirit and the letter thereof, should return most fervent thanks to the divine mercy ; but by no means rise up to judge her sisters. Such presumption could not escape chastisement ; God would punish her by humbling her ; her vain thoughts might even lead her to destruction. Let her hold to the word and example of the same St. Paul, who says of himself: *Forgetting the things that are behind, and stretching forth myself to those that are before, I press towards the mark, to the prize.*[3]

Let her keep her holy mother St Angela, constantly before her as a model ; and let her

---

[1] Prov. xix. 16.   [2] 1 Cor. x. 12.

[3] Phil. iii. 13, 14

remember that as a follower of Jesus Christ, she is bound to advance continually in virtue by the words: *Be ye perfect, as your heavenly Father is perfect.*[1]

She who meditates this will never have cause for elation of mind, or for thinking herself perfect ; but she will feel convinced that God has still demands on us, even when we have done all that we could do: *When you have done all these things that are commanded you, say: We are unprofitable servants ; we have done that which we ought to do.*[2] And we have done it by means of thy help, Lord. *Wherefore, not to us, but to Thy Name belongs the glory.*[3]

If, on the contrary, some one should find in the mirror of this Rule and its Commentary, her own imperfections, and her backwardness in many respects, let her not lose courage.

She has but to recommence with new confidence, this confidence being placed, not in herself, but in God. Her zeal for perfection must now be the greater, in proportion as she has been longer in default, according to the word of the Apostle : *Redeeming the time.*[4] Yes,

---

[1] St. Matt. v. 48. [2] St. Luke, xvii. 10. [3] Ps. cxiii.
[4] Ephes. v. 16.

Spouse of Jesus Christ, redeem the time! Hours, days, months, years of grace, are lost for you; you failed to employ them as you could, and ought to have done. Therefore, redeem the time; retrieve it, by ever new and increasing fervour. It is not yet too late. *But, behold the night cometh, when no man can work.*[1] It has not however actually come, you breathe still, and you can if you wish it, in *a short space fulfil a long time.*[2]

At last then, resolve! With all your heart exclaim: Lord, I have said it: *Now I begin. This is the change of the right hand of the Most High.*[3] My Jesus, Thou dost *stand at the gate* of my heart, *and knock,*[4] by Thy grace, and Thou also sayest: *To-day, if thou shalt hear my voice harden not thy heart.*[5] *Speak, Lord, thy servant heareth!*[6] *Lord, what wilt Thou have me to do?*[7]

Oh! yes, I have heard, and I am resolved to obey. I must keep my holy Rule, and follow the example of my blessed Mother, St. Angela.

---

[1] St. John, ix. 4   [2] Wis. iv. 13.   [3] Ps. lxxvi. 11.
[4] Apoc. iii. 20.   [5] Ps. xciv. 8.   [6] 1 Kings, iii. 9.
[7] Acts, ix. 6.

Yes, Lord, I am resolved! But help Thou my weakness. With Thy grace I can do all!

Happy you who speak thus to the Lord God, for it is written: *Peace and mercy on those who keep this Rule.*[1]

My Sisters, may the grace of our Lord Jesus Christ be with you all. Amen.

[1] Gal. vi. 16.

A. M. D. G.

M. H. Gill & Son, Printers, Dublin.

www.ingramcontent.com/pod-product-compliance
Lightning Source LLC
Chambersburg PA
CBHW030121030726
47498CB00007B/2493

9783744659345